Managing Successful Projects

A Handbook for All Managers

■

PHILIP BAGULEY

the Institute
of Management

FOUNDATION

PITMAN
PUBLISHING

PITMAN PUBLISHING
128 Long Acre, London WC2E 9AN

A Division of Pearson Professional Limited

First published in Great Britain 1995

British Library Cataloguing in Publication Data
A CIP catalogue record for this book can be obtained
from the British Library.

ISBN 0 273 61892 X cased
3 5 7 9 10 8 6 4 2
ISBN 0 273 61344 Paperback
3 5 7 9 10 8 6 4 2

Typeset by PanTek Arts
Printed and bound in Great Britain by
Bell and Bain Ltd, Glasgow

*The Publishers' policy is to use paper manufactured
from sustainable forests.*

Contents

■

Acknowledgements

∎

The insights, ideas, experiences and influences which come together to form a book often accumulate slowly and are gradually refined by the rough and tumble of day to day life. For this reason thanks are due to all those people with and for whom I have managed, consulted, lectured and tutored in the past – in one way or another they have all contributed to this book. Acknowledgement is also due for the help and support given by my agent, Teresa Chris, Mark Allin and Richard Stagg of Pitman Publishing and my partner, Linda Baguley, whose counsel and support were, yet again, given so generously during the creation of the text.

1

Introduction

What do Noah's ark, the Concorde supersonic plane, the pyramids, becoming a quality organisation and installing a new automatic beverage vending machine all have in common? They are all examples of the art of project management, and this book is about that process of managing projects *and doing it successfully.*

As we move towards the end of the twentieth century, significant change has become a regular, almost common, feature of all of our working lives. Many of these changes take on the form of 'projects' and these are often managed and controlled by managers whose experience and skills have been acquired in the management of regular, repetitive day to day operations. But, as we will see in this book, all projects are unique, and for this and other reasons they demand, if they are to be successfully managed, a blend of skills which is significantly different from those used in the management of day to day operations.

Aims and objectives

The aim of this book is to provide you, as the actual or aspiring manager of a project, with an introduction to the ways in which that project can be efficiently and effectively managed. When you have read this book you should know:

■ what a project is
■ how to successfully plan, manage and control a project
■ how to ensure that project contributes to the survival and success of the organisation
■ how to begin, with confidence, the process of managing your own projects.

Style, content and structure

This book is not a textbook, nor is it a book which deals, as many books on project management do, exclusively with the management of

1

large and complex civil engineering or manufacturing projects. Instead, it is a book based on the reality that many, many projects:

- are small to medium in size
- often involve outcomes with little or limited tangibility, such as influencing or changing attitudes, improving performance, restructuring organisations or departments, etc.
- are managed by managers who do not have (or need) a technical or engineering background.

Neither is it a book to be read through at one sitting and then forgotten, but a book to dipped into, referred to and browsed over so that you, the reader, will continue to use it as your experience and skill in the management of projects grow. Its contents are practical and focused on the achievement of results, with the text based on useful ideas and pointers to appropriate methods and tools – all of which are aimed at enabling you to develop and enhance your ability to manage projects. Many of your projects will be modest or even small in scope or cost, and particular attention will be paid to the management of these small projects such as those which abound during the process of performance improvement and in which managers – often on a part-time basis – are frequently involved.

Each of the 14 chapters focuses on a particular aspect of the exciting and rewarding process of managing projects, starting with an introductory chapter which looks at the nature, characteristics and variety of the project and compares and contrasts these with the day to day management tasks with which so many managers are familiar. This chapter also identifies the key project issues of time, cost, outcome achievement and outcome quality. Later chapters go on to look at how to:

- evaluate and choose
- organise
- plan
- lead
- monitor
- control projects.

All projects have change as an objective and the management of change, the teams which are key to the success of that process and the ways in which you, as a project manager, can manage the problems and conflicts which are often consequences of the change process are all the subjects of individual chapters. The book draws to a close by looking at the often neglected art of closing a project, then reviews the key aspects of successful project management and provides a glossary of project terms with simple and brief explanations. All of these chapters close with a summary to remind you of the key points, and many of them contain self-assessment questionnaires.

Who is this book for?

For many managers, the process of project management represents just one of a number of tools which they can use to solve problems or create change. Despite this reality many of the texts on this subject assume either that readers have a career investment in being a project manager or that it is a role that they carry out frequently. This book is written for the larger, more varied and more universal group of managers for whom project management is an occasional, infrequent or even part-time task. Even so, despite their universality, the needs of these managers differ. They may, for example, need:

- to begin to develop the skills of effective project management so that they can manage more efficiently – whatever their seniority and whatever the size or purpose of their organisation
- to help others, as a mentor or a manager, to develop the skills of effective project management
- to begin to develop the skills of effective project management as a part of a professional training programme or course.

All of these managers, and others with differing, perhaps more unique, needs, are welcome on the journey that we will take through the pages of this book – a journey which will lead all of us to the point at which we can effectively and efficiently choose, manage and close our own projects.

3

2

Projects – their nature and purpose

Overview

The first step in our journey to successful project management is to take a look at what we mean by a 'project'. This chapter looks at the nature, characteristics and variety of the project and compares and contrasts the way in which projects are managed with the day to day management tasks with which we are all familiar.

Objectives

When you have read this chapter, you should:
- know what are the key characteristics of all projects
- understand the differences between projects and day to day management
- have a basic definition which we can apply to all projects
- have grasped the idea of the project life cycle.

Projects – common or unusual?

Man's earliest projects were about the creation of massive structures such as Noah's ark, the Tower of Babel, Stonehenge or the pyramids and were rare, once in a life time events. In the 1990s, projects are becoming an increasingly common feature of all our lives and particularly of the organisations in which we work and which create our products and services. This increasing presence has come about for two reasons. The first of these is the growing realisation that the project can be a powerful management tool – one which enhances the ability of managers to plan, direct and execute the ways in which organisational resources are used. As such, a well conceived and managed project can make major contributions to both the efficiency and the effectiveness of all organisations, whatever their objectives and whatever the products or services that they generate. The second reason is to do with the increasing competitiveness and volatility of the environment within which all of our organisations function. In order to survive and grow in this hostile and demanding climate, organisations need to develop and use the ability to react and respond quickly to the needs of their customers. The project is a proven and effective way of doing this and upgrading the ability of any organisation to respond effectively and efficiently to these needs.

Projects – large or small?

Despite this increasing use of projects it is evident that many of the projects with which we are all familiar are concerned with large, expensive and well publicised outcomes. Modern examples of this type of project include the Russian sputnik space project, the American 'Man on the Moon' project, the Concorde supersonic plane, the Channel Tunnel and the Aswan dam. But not all of our projects are massive, multi-billion pound or dollar, decade-long endeavours involving the creation of massive or highly sophisticated technological artefacts. The projects which our organisations often implement are concerned with shorter duration and less costly activities such as the launch of a new product, the reduction of new product introduction lead times, the 're-imaging' of shops or other retail outlets, or the relocation of offices or other facilities.

Projects – buildings or ideas?

These projects are not only concerned with tangible physical outcomes but might also involve the gathering of information, the changing of the structures of their own or other organisations, and influencing the views or behaviour of others. Examples of these influencing projects include advertising campaigns designed to persuade us to buy particular products and those campaigns designed to persuade us to moderate the amount of alcohol that we drink or to change our diet and take exercise to reduce the risk of heart disease. The projects of the organisations in which we work are often aimed at changing the ways in which we do things. For example, the key process of enhancing efficiency is, for many of our organisations, seen to be an ongoing and continuous one, consisting of small, incremental steps. However, there are also occasions and circumstances where it is necessary to take a large step, or even a leap, forward. These large steps are often called projects and can vary considerably in size, cost and duration. They can, for example, be concerned with change in the physical resources that those organisations use, such as the building of a new office block or factory, or concerned with changes in procedures and methods such as the introduction of a quality manual based on BS 5750. They can also be concerned with influencing people in order to change their behaviour or views and opinions, such as in a Total Quality Management (TQM) campaign, or with distributing information, as in a 'this is how we have done' company annual results report. At the lower end of the size and/or cost scale, these projects might be concerned with the design and introduction of a new training programme, the installation of a beverage vending machine or the modification of a record form.

6

Projects – work or play?

Our experience of these projects is not limited to the places or organisations in which we work, for we have all had, and will continue to have, projects which reflect our own individual needs and wants. These projects can, for example, be concerned with our own or our children's education, the location and features of our homes, what kind of car we drive, how well we swim, dance, run or play golf – or any other aspect of our lives. They can result in our moving house, having an extension built, organising a holiday or even choosing and buying a new suit or dress.

All projects that on earth do dwell

By now we can see that projects can be concerned with any aspect of our lives and that these projects can:

- be of any size from small to large
- take days or decades to complete
- involve costs from tens to billions of pounds
- have outcomes which are either tangible or intangible
- involve any number of people, from individuals to nations.

And yet, despite the rich diversity evident in the range of their outcomes, size, cost and duration, all of these projects do have a number of characteristics in common. Faced with the considerable variety of these projects, it does seem to be asking a lot of you to accept that *all* projects, whether concerned with building a new factory, buying a new suit or persuading people to behave in different ways, have a number of limited but nevertheless common characteristics. That is the case, however, and what we need to do now is to identify what these common characteristics are.

1 All projects involve people

Projects are people-centred – they need and demand, whatever their duration or outcomes, the skills and abilities of people in order to create, plan and manage the processes and activities involved. These people and their skills and abilities enable the detail of both the course and content of the project to adapt and change in the face of the vagaries of the 'real' world. Without them the project would become an empty and meaningless husk containing little of its original intent, energy or brilliance. But projects share this people-centred characteristic with the day to day routine operations which take place in all our organisations – they too, if they are to be carried out successfully, need and demand the skills and abilities of those involved. However, as we shall see shortly, the demands of projects are different, in both content and magnitude, to the demands of our day to day routine activities.

7

2 All projects are, in some way, unique

Every project has, at its core, features which are unique to that project. In some projects the influence of those unique features will be considerable and they will be singular, one-off events while other projects will display lesser degrees of uniqueness. For example, the construction of the Thames Flood Barrier was a wholly unique project which will not be repeated elsewhere, while a project to build standard dwelling houses outside Chester will limit its uniqueness to those factors associated with that particular site. That is to say that while the houses built may be of a standard design and are not unique, the site is unique and will have its own characteristics, which will include shape, size, drainage and access, etc. Similarly, a project to restructure the social services department of a local authority will be wholly unique in that it will reflect, among other things, the current political and economic environment, the numbers, location and needs of its unique set of clients and the skills, availability and experience of its unique group of staff. Nevertheless, a project to enhance the effectiveness of a team within that department will result in outcomes which are capable of application elsewhere, despite the uniqueness of the team's composition and workload. So all projects are, in some way and to greater or lesser extents, unique. In this respect they differ considerably from the repetitive day to day activities of our organisations.

3 All projects exist for a limited and defined period of time

All projects have defined deadlines or target completion dates. This means that the project has a limited life span – it does not go on for ever – and will reach a point in time when it is complete. When this point is reached the project ceases to exist – its management team will disband and move on to other projects – and the outcome will be handed over to those who will manage its day to day operation. On larger and more complex projects, this life span might cover several years, but even these projects will reach an end-point. This characteristic also contrasts strongly with the repetitive and continuing day to day operational activities of our organisations.

4 All projects are primarily concerned with change

While the day to day operations of our organisations are primarily concerned with continuity, predictability and stability, the activities of a project are almost exclusively concerned with change – with knocking down the old and building up the new. As we will see in Chapter 9, the skills required to manage this environment of change are quite different from those needed to maintain the relative stability and predictability of the organisation's day to day operations.

5 All projects have defined outcomes or targets

All projects have well defined goals, targets or sets of desired results. These might be, for example, the completion of the building of a house or the publication of a book. They are often divided into sub-goals or sub-tasks, which, as we will see in Chapter 5, help the planning, control and management of the project. Often these sub-tasks are interdependent – that is they each require other tasks to be completed before they in turn can be completed – and they must all be concluded in order to achieve the goal or project outcome.

6 All projects are undertaken by the use of a variety of resources

One of the key characteristics of a project is the way in which it uses its resources. For example, a project to reduce community crime levels will require information on the nature and location of past crimes and those who were involved both as victims and perpetrators, and will demand the ability to analyse that information. This project will also require know-how about the social patterns and idiosyncrasies of the community, what is feasible and acceptable in terms of preventative activities, and the resources available to police it. Each of these resources can be contained in a different person and will be required at different stages of the project, and their use will be fleeting and short-lived. Similarly, a project for the erection of a house will require periods of activity from bricklayers, electricians, joiners, tilers, plasterers and painters. These periods of activity will rarely overlap with each other but they will depend upon each other. For example, the painter cannot start his activities until the joiner, the plasterer and the tiler have completed theirs. They, in turn, cannot start their activities until the electrician has completed his or her activities, and so on. The transitory nature of these resources is present also in the equipment needed for the projects – in this case, the diggers, scaffolding, cranes, etc. In a well managed project these will appear when needed – not before – and will be taken away when their task is complete. This also contrasts strongly with the fixed nature of the resources used in the day to day operational activities of our organisations.

9

Projects and day to day activities

As we can see from the above, the characteristics of a project are quite different from those of the routine day to day activities of our organisations. Projects have defined end-points and outcomes and are concerned with uniqueness, change and the use of transient resources, while the routine, day to day operations of our organisations are concerned with stability, continuity and repetition. One way of illustrating these significant differences is shown overleaf.

Projects and day to day tasks

These differences mean that projects are:

- unique
- use transient resources
- have defined endpoints
- about creating change.

In contrast, our day to day activities are about:

- repetition and replication
- stability
- using fixed resources.

Because of these differences, projects:

- are different from the other activities that we carry out in our organisations
- must be organised, planned and managed in ways which differ from those that we use in our day to day activities.

These differences mean that projects, if they are to be successful, demand the use of different approaches and skills in their management. Later chapters in this book will take a look at how projects are:

- structured
- managed
- planned
- controlled
- closed.

You can explore some of the differences between your routine tasks and your projects by using the project check list below.

PROJECT CHECK LIST

1 Think of a job or task that you have recently completed.

2 Write down, in a single sentence, what you achieved by completing that job.

3 Answer the following questions about the job.

Did it have a defined start date?	Yes ☐ No ☐
Did it have a defined end date?	Yes ☐ No ☐
Did it involve you and other people?	Yes ☐ No ☐
Did it involve changing something?	Yes ☐ No ☐
Did the task have a clear and well defined outcome?	Yes ☐ No ☐
Was the outcome of the task unusual?	Yes ☐ No ☐

If yes, was it unusual because
– it had not been done before?　　　　Yes ☐ No ☐
– you hadn't done it before?　　　　　Yes ☐ No ☐
– it was unique?　　　　　　　　　　Yes ☐ No ☐

Did the task involve people with a range of different skills?　　　　　　　Yes ☐ No ☐

Key: If you accumulate seven or more yes's then you had a project, five or fewer yes's and you had a routine task. Between five and seven yes's probably means that you've not clearly defined the job – or have a very unusual routine task.

Projects – a definition

Our review of the characteristics of all projects should, by now, have brought us to the point where we can begin to think about a simple and condensed definition of what makes a project. When we start to look at what other people have said and written it is not surprising, in the light of the considerable variety of projects created by our organisations, to find that our language and, more specifically, the literature of project management contain a variety of definitions for projects. For example, a typical dictionary provides a simple and basic definition, telling us that a project is 'a plan or a scheme'. Other definitions stress the uncertainty which is involved in some projects and typically tell us about 'risk', 'uncertainty' and 'steps into the unknown'. Further definitions speak eloquently of 'human endeavour', while others speak of specific outcomes or simply beginnings and ends.

But none of these really captures the essence of a project, which, as we saw earlier, embodies uniqueness and definitive statements about duration and outcomes. From this point onwards the definition that we shall use is a simple and straightforward one which tells us that a project is:

12

a sequence of activities which are:
- **connected**
- **conducted over a limited period of time**
- **targeted to generate a unique but well defined outcome.**

When we apply this definition to the examples of projects given earlier in this chapter, we find that they all fit – they all display a degree of uniqueness, consist of activities which are connected to each other and have defined outcomes and limited time spans. This means that we can view the project and its management as a tool to be used in order to achieve any outcome that:

- is unique or one-off in nature
- can be defined
- needs to be achieved within a specified time period.

This means, for example, that we can use a project to :

- reorganise our company or department
- improve our organisation's performance
- introduce a new way of doing things
- get rid of an old way of doing things
- influence the ways in which people think or feel about something.

Question: **When is a project not a project ?**
Answer: **When it's a regular day to day event.**

But the project is only one of many tools which managers use, and they must understand not only *when* to use it but also, and perhaps more importantly, *how* to use it. To ensure that we take the next step on our journey towards that knowledge we need to identify the key dimensions of all these projects.

Projects – the key dimensions

Many managers fall into the trap of thinking about a project only in terms of its outcome or performance. For example, we might think of a project involving the rearrangement of an office only in terms of the outcome of the relocated desks and other furniture. However, the outcomes of this and indeed all projects have other dimensions. We might ask, for example, questions about:

■ how long did the rearrangement take?
■ how much did it cost?
■ were the furniture and desks moved to the positions we wanted?
■ did the rearrangement achieve want we wanted it to?

These other dimensions of the project can also exert a significant influence upon the efficiency and the effectiveness of the project process. As a result, when we define, manage, plan, monitor and control a project we need to do so by taking account of all of the four interrelated key dimensions of that project. Traditional project management has, however, focused on the only three complementary dimensions:

■ the nature of the outcomes or performance
■ the time taken or needed to achieve that performance
■ the costs of all the resources used in the project.

However, at the end of the twentieth century, the presence and influence of the Quality Revolution with its accent on the provision of customer satisfaction means that we now have to add a fourth and also complementary dimension – the quality or 'fitness for purpose' of the project outcome.

For example, a project concerned with the building of a house would, traditionally, be defined only in terms of its:

■ **performance** – number and size of rooms, shape, facilities, capacity, etc., as in four bed, two bath, timber frame ranch house with patio, outdoor swimming pool and barbecue

- **cost** – £150,000
- **duration** – to be ready for use by 1 December 1999.

The additional and fourth dimension of quality relates the project to the needs of the customer and will be expressed in terms of both individual and idiosyncratic factors. These will be both objective, such as 'Is the bath big enough for two adults?', and subjective, such as 'Does the house feel right?'. Those of you who have undertaken the project of house hunting will recognise the importance of this subjective factor and the power of its influence upon your decision taking.

These four dimensions of time, cost, performance and quality are *the* key dimensions for all projects. As such they must be:

- clearly defined at the beginning of the project
- monitored throughout its duration
- carefully managed and controlled at all times.

Indeed, the importance of these factors is such that it can be argued that the failure to define all four at the beginning of the project will result in an unsuccessful project. These dimensions are both connected to and dependent upon each other, as is shown below:

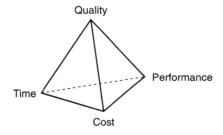

The key project dimensions

For example, a shortage of time left to complete a project might be compensated for by taking on extra labour – at additional cost – or reducing the work content by changing the outcome or performance. Similarly, an increase in the performance or quality dimensions of the project may require increases in both time and money to compensate.

The project life cycle

It is also evident that however well defined the desired outcomes might be, the project process itself is, like all human endeavours, subject to

14

change, growth and decline. Projects grow, from small beginnings, to become large and impressive undertakings that mature and ultimately die. This pattern of growth and decline is a familiar one which we see in the life cycles of many organic systems or organisms. The life cycle idea is also commonly used in management literature, with examples from marketing that describe the variations in sales volumes over the life of a product, and from quality assurance that describe how product reliability varies with age. It can also be applied to the project. In its simplest form, the stages of the project life cycle are:

- **Conception.** During this stage the project is identified, its feasibility reviewed and initial estimates of cost generated. This stage will also involve an initial definition of performance and time. The end of this stage, during which the project is compared with other projects or standards of performance, will be marked by a decision to implement the project - or not. The decision to implement will lead to the next stage of growth while a decision not to proceed will lead to the death of the project. Many projects die at this stage and Chapter 3 describes how that decision can be made.
- **Birth and development.** During this stage the detailed design of the project outcome is developed and decisions are made about who will do what and when. Cost and time estimates are also refined. Both this and the earlier stage involve a relatively low, though accelerating pace of activity.
- **Adulthood.** This is the stage in which the planned work takes place. It is also the stage with the highest activity rate and as such it requires effective monitoring, control and forecasting procedures which will tell the project manager what has or hasn't been done or spent, what ought to have been done or spent, and what will need to be done or spent in the future. At the end of this stage the project will have reached completion and the outcome should have been handed over to those who will use it.
- **Old age and termination.** This stage involves a slower pace of activity, involving the review and audit of the project and, ultimately, the break up of the project team.

These life cycle stages are illustrated overleaf.

But not only does what is done change throughout this cycle, the rates at which things are done also change. This means that the demands and needs for resources or effort that each of the life cycle stages has will be different from each other and will wax and wane within each stage. For most projects, the adulthood stage, with its

15

focus on getting things done, involves the peak level of resource demands, as illustrated in the resource usage graph below.

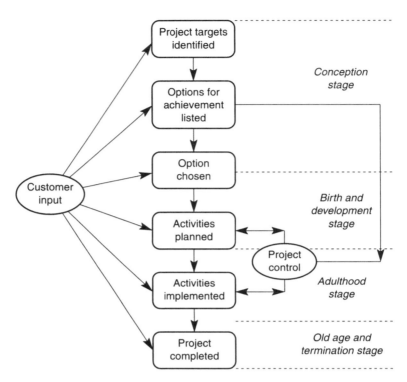

The project lifecycle

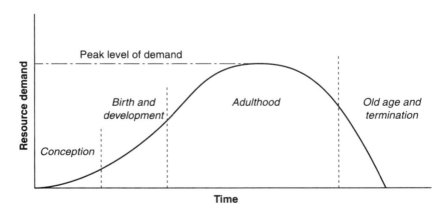

Project resource demands

Time, cost, performance or quality?

There are also other more subtle, but just as important, changes which take place as the project moves through its life cycle from conception to death. These other changes are concerned with the relative importance of the four project dimensions of time, cost, performance and quality. During the conception stage all of these will have equal importance, but once we move into the birth and development stage time begins to edge ahead of performance with cost and quality taking third place. This probably reflects the fact that most of the scheduling and planning decisions are taken during this stage. Throughout most of the adulthood stage, performance will be the key issue, but by the end of this stage all of these dimensions will have assumed equal importance and this ranking will continue throughout the final old age and termination stage.

Question: **Which stage of the project life cycle demands the maximum resources?**
Answer: **Adulthood.**

Managing projects

The process of management is often seen as a juggling act, one in which the manager struggles to keep aloft or balance the often conflicting needs of, among others, the organisation, the customer and his or her staff. The skilful day to day manager will trade off between the dimensions of time, performance, quality and cost in order to satisfy these needs. But as we saw earlier in this chapter, one of the characteristics of a project is the presence of a finite time scale for its completion. As a consequence, the freedom of the project manager to trade off time against money, performance or quality is far more limited than that of a day to day manager.

One of the ways in which the process of project management can be viewed is to see it as a conversion process during which the completed process is created from a variety of inputs:

- **information** – about time scales, cost, performance, quality and the client

- **people** – with their skills, needs, experience and abilities
- **resources** – of materials, money and time.

The process which converts these can be illustrated as shown below.

The project inputs

When we probe into the 'box' at the centre of this process what we find is that the role of the project manager is key to the success of that transformation process. We will examine this role in more detail in Chapter 6 but at this point we need to note that the project manager has to balance the demands of:

18

- the client
- the project
- the project team.

However, this juggling act is not carried out in a vacuum. The choice of the project to be implemented is influenced by the needs and goals of both the client organisation (see Chapter 3) and the project organisation (see Chapter 4), and contributions and support are provided by the ways in which the project is organised (see Chapter 4), planned (see Chapter 5) and managed (see Chapter 9).

The project manager must also ensure that the project integrity is maintained by balancing the conflicts, arguments and rivalries which can easily lead to an erosion of the original definition of the project outcome, cost and duration (see Chapter 11) and by solving the problems which spring up like toadstools along the project's journey to completion (see Chapter 10). As the leader of the project team the project manager must also lead and motivate his or her team of project staff who:

- will only be members of that team for the duration of the project
- may have been 'borrowed' from other departments or functions.

The project manager's role as a team leader will also need to cover the selection of that team – to ensure that the relevant functional skills are present – and the transfer, at the end of the project, of these team members into other roles (see Chapters 7 and 13). The complexity and often conflicting nature of these tasks, together with the need to be able to manage what are often considerable but fluctuating levels of resources (see Chapters 8 and 12), mean that the project manager's job demands a rare mix of skills and abilities. Finally, this highly skilled juggling act must be closed and the project completed in such a way as to ensure that the experience gained is available for use in other projects (see Chapter 13).

The management of projects, as we will see in the following chapters, represents a demanding but satisfying task which can make a major contribution to the capability of all organisations to ride out the storms of change which sweep through the environment of the 1990s.

Summary

■ *The project is a very common way of creating change and as such it has a very wide range of outcomes, which can be tangible and/or intangible.*

■ *Projects can:*
  – be large or small
  – involve any number of people
  – last for days or years.

■ *All projects:*
  – involve people
  – are unique
  – are concerned with change
  – have defined outcomes and end-points
  – use a variety of transitory resources.

■ *A project can be defined as a sequence of activities which are:*
  – connected
  – conducted over a limited period of time
  – targeted to generate a unique but well defined outcome.

■ *All projects have a life cycle with the stages of:*
  – conception
  – birth and development
  – adulthood
  – old age and termination.

■ *Each of these project life cycle stages has different rates of activity and resource demands.*

■ *The successful project manager uses a rare mix of skills and ability.*

19

Choosing your project

Overview

The key first step in the management of a successful project is the selection of the 'right' project. That choice is often made from a number of potential projects and this chapter looks at the ways in which it can be made and the factors that influence it.

Objectives

By the end of this chapter you should have a better understanding of:
- **risk and uncertainty**
- **the connections between the objectives of the organisation and those of the project**
- **how and when to use numerical evaluation processes**
- **how and when to use non-numerical evaluation processes.**

Risk and uncertainty

All projects are about change and that process of change has a two-way action, carrying with it both the opportunity for us to grasp success and the risk that we might experience failure. Successful projects are not only managed, planned and controlled with skill and efficiency, they are also chosen with care and thought and with a clear understanding of the risks involved. These risks expose us to 'mischance or peril' and their roots lie deep in the uncertainties which often abound in our workplaces. But uncertainty, like birth and death, will always be with us and we will never be able to eliminate it. There will always be alternatives that we haven't thought of, foreseen or predicted and limitations to the amount or quality of information on which we base our decisions. For example, when we launch a new product we face uncertainty about whether that product will sell or not and we put at risk the investments that we make in plant, materials and time in order to create that product. Similarly, when we reorganise the work or office spaces that we and our teams use we face the uncertainty about whether the revised layout will be as effective as the old one and put at risk the investment that we made in time, labour and money in order to achieve that reorganisation. But uncertainty and risk aren't always negative in their implications. Facing the uncertainties and risks that others turn away from can be both exciting and rewarding and can lead to considerable success. Our new product may be a runaway success or our new office layout enable us to reach new peaks of customer service – but they can never be free from risk.

Definitions

Uncertainty: **The lack of information about the duration, occurrence or value of future events.**

Risk: **The estimated degree of uncertainty.**

21

Risk – revolution or evolution?

For many of us the risks that we encounter in our day to day lives are risks that have evolved slowly. This evolution almost always takes place as a series of small, additive changes and our exposure to the consequent risks is often governed by the laws of chance. A classic and common example of this is the experience of driving in traffic. The risks associated with this have increased gradually as the levels of both traffic and traffic speed have increased over the years. Our individual responses to these rising risk levels have also often been implemented gradually and might have included driving more defensively or undertaking our journeys at different times of the day. Our projects, however, do not represent sequences of gradual change – they are quantum leaps or step changes and as such are revolutionary rather than evolutionary in their nature.

These projects represent deliberate and chosen step changes in:

■ the ways in which we do things
■ what we do them with.

As a consequence our risk levels will also undergo similar step changes. One of the key actions in managing a successful project is to ensure that the consequent changes in risk are acceptable and tolerable. In order to achieve this we need to evaluate them as rigorously as we can. However, that process cannot eliminate these risks. We still, since our projects are unique, have to take that journey into the unknown. But others have made this journey before us and what we must now do is look at how they have achieved success.

Reducing the risk

Since we cannot eradicate risk and uncertainty from our projects then what we must do, if we are to achieve success, is to limit their influence upon those projects. In order to do that we need to :

- identify the type, level and source of foreseeable risk
- take necessary steps (if possible) to reduce or eliminate that risk
- decide whether or not we will accept that risk.

This three stage sequence is an integral part of the larger process of project evaluation and selection, often used to examine a number of alternative projects and then enable us to choose which one we wish to implement. The first step in reducing the risk level of our projects is to identify the nature and source of risk. One way of doing this is to use a risk matrix.

| | | Project outcome | |
		Been done before	Never been done before
Project change process	Been done before	Low risk	Moderate risk
	Never been done before	Moderate risk	High risk

The risk matrix

This matrix tells us that if our project involves doing something that no one else has ever done before and doing it in ways that have never been used before, then we have a high risk project. The causes of that risk are the uncertainty about the success of the project process and the success of the outcome, if it is achieved. When we use proven methods in our projects or have project outcomes that have, in one form or another, been achieved before, then we reduce the risk levels of our projects. So if we choose to build a house using novel, high tech materials such as carbon fibres and to do so from the roof downwards rather than the foundations upwards, then we have a high risk project. If, however, we decide to use conventional material or to build it from the bottom up, then the risk lessens; and if we do both, then we have a low risk project. Similarly, we will incur risk if we try to improve the efficiency of our work team by holding communal meditation sessions in the lunch break or by sending them all on holiday together. While both of these may work, they also involve the risk that they may not work and consequently result in lower team morale or efficiency.

Chance and consequences

When we have identified the cause and level of risk in our project, we then need to look at the consequences of that risk. Many managers would argue that if we are to do that then we need to know all the facts, details and implications of the risk before we can evaluate its effects. But this is not always so and we first need to look at:

- the chance or probability of the risk occurring
- the risk's potential consequences.

For example, a high probability risk is one that we are likely to need to know more about because it is more likely to happen, while a low probability risk would appear to be less demanding in terms of data needs. However, this picture can and does change when we look at the consequences of the risk. For example, a risk which is likely to occur only once every hundred years would appear to be one that would not demand much of our attention. If, however, when that risk occurs it results in the deaths of two million people, then it will warrant and receive more attention. This marriage of the risk probability and the consequences of that risk if it occurrs is an important one. It will give us, even if we have to estimate or guess both the consequence and the frequency, a basis on which we can decide whether or not to attempt to reduce the risk. For example, if this product of probability and consequence is high then we will need further data in order to define the risk. If the product is low we can then either:

- decide on a strategy from the data we have
- ignore the risk until either its probability increases or it acquires greater consequences.

If this product of chance and consequence is high and we decide to get more information about that risk then we need to be looking at the answers to such questions as:

- how much data do we have now?
- how much more data can we get and at what cost?

The scope and outcomes of this information-gathering need to reflect both:

- the anticipated value of outcomes – why spend more money on gathering information than we will gain in increased profit?
- the quality and accuracy of the information – why spend time and money on evaluating gossip?

Reducing the risk

The next step in our process of choosing a project is to attempt to reduce the level of that risk. As we saw earlier, high risk follows our use of an untried project change process to generate a novel project outcome. We also saw that we can reduce the level of that risk by using a tried and proven change process and/or generating a tried project outcome. But this is not always possible and some of our projects will require us to push back the boundaries of technology or experience. We may need, for example, to use new and unproved processes in order to gain or maintain market leadership, or we may choose to try new ways of doing things because the old ways either don't work or produce the results that we require. One of the ways to lessen that risk is to use a risk check list (see opposite).

Another of the ways in which that risk can be lessened is by the use of feasibility studies. These usually involve small multi-discipli-nary teams of two or three people and have the objective of answering such questions as:

- how long will it really take?
- is it possible?
- how much will it cost?

A good feasibility study will weed out bad or faulty ideas, identify 'dead ends', and produce a clear assessment of risk and benefit together with recommendations about the next step. That next step may include a further evaluation of the risks involved and this can be done by the use of prototypes and/or trials. A prototype usually

---

RISK CHECK LIST

1 Project Outcome

Does it:
- consist of a new product or service?   Yes ☐ No ☐
- use new and untried techniques?   Yes ☐ No ☐
- use new and untried technology?   Yes ☐ No ☐
- include non-essential items?   Yes ☐ No ☐
- keep you awake at night worrying whether it will
  be successful?   Yes ☐ No ☐

Is it:
- complex and/or sophisticated?   Yes ☐ No ☐
- likely to appeal to a minority of users?   Yes ☐ No ☐

2 Project change process

Does it :
- ignore prior successful experience?   Yes ☐ No ☐
- not have the ability to cope successfully with
  change and unexpected risk?   Yes ☐ No ☐
- use non-standard items of equipment?   Yes ☐ No ☐
- use a new and untried combination of standard
  items of equipment?   Yes ☐ No ☐
- make you anxious about what will happen next? Yes ☐ No ☐

Key: If you have more than four yes's, then you have a moderate risk
project. If you have more than six, then you have a high risk project.

---

consists of a first attempt to create the project outcome, while a trial
consists of exposing the prototype project outcome or the project
process to 'friendly' users. For example, a project to build a dam may
involve the use of modular concrete 'building bricks'. The risk
involved in producing those components on an assembly line can be
evaluated by a trial of a prototype assembly line whose products are
thoroughly tested. Similarly, a project to change the ways in which
information about students is recorded and upgraded may involve the
generation of a prototype new record form and its trial on one course
or programme. While prototypes and trials both cost money they can
be cheaper than the failure that might occur if they were not used.

All of these actions will provide us with:

- more information about the risks of our projects
- the opportunity to reduce those risks.

Evaluate the positive, eliminate the negative

Once we have identified the source and level of risk and done what we can to reduce its level, what we must then do is decide whether that risk and its financial and other implications are acceptable. Project evaluation and selection techniques are both numerical and non-numerical in nature and are versatile enough to be used in a wide variety of situations. We can, for example, make our choice by calculating the period of time needed to pay back the initial capital investment, or by using sophisticated accounting concepts such as net present value. We may also use non-numerical techniques that allow us to express our intuition or preferences. We can, for example, use these techniques to decide which of several makes and types of washing machine we wish to purchase for our home, which size, type and make of delivery van to purchase for our small business, which research project to invest in or which site on which to locate our new factory. Under all of these circumstances each of the choices (or projects) that we face will have different costs, benefits and risks and these will rarely be known with certainty or accuracy. The factors which affect each of these projects and our choice of which one to implement are often not limited to those involved in the project itself. Other influences such as legislation, interest rates, the actions of competitors and the industrial relations climate of our organisations can also play a significant part in the choice process. All of these and other factors are brought to bear upon our choice of which project we implement and that choice is, as we saw earlier, a key step in the process of managing a successful project.

How do we choose?

The techniques that we use to evaluate and select our projects can be numerical or non-numerical in nature. But whatever their source or type, the techniques that we use to aid our choice of project must be:

26

- easy to use
- inexpensive in relation to the cost of the project
- flexible and able to respond to changes
- consistent in their operation
- capable of generating results that are understood and accepted
- seen to be realistic both in terms of the input data that they need and the manner in which that data is used.

All of these techniques must also, if they are to contribute to the success of our project, enable us to choose a project which contributes to our organisation's well-being and survival. For profit-making organisations this will be measured in terms of:

- profitability
- competitive position
- efficient use of resources.

However, many of our non-profit-making organisations are also increasingly pressured to move towards self-funding or to maximise their use of scarce resources. Their successful projects will contribute to issues such as:

- effective allocation of scarce or expensive resources like capital or people
- making sure that those resources are both efficiently and effectively used in the organisation's operations.

Objectives – project and organisation

Whatever the objectives of our projects, they must, if they are to succeed, be compatible with the principal aims and objectives of our organisations and the goals of other projects. The objectives of our organisations are often encapsulated in what is called the strategy of the organisation. This strategy is about the organisation's future, and its objectives will be about:

- the whole of the organisation rather than its parts
- the long term rather than the medium or short term
- the broad scope of that organisation's activities.

If our projects do not demonstrate compatibility with these strategic organisational objectives, they invite not only failure, but also rejection. One way of avoiding this pitfall and of achieving this

compatibility is to generate and use hierarchies of objectives or objective trees. These consist of structured diagrams of linked and desired
objectives and can help to identify conflicts between organisational
objectives and those of the project. They can also help to recognise
conflicts between individual projects. The outline of part of an objective tree for an organisational objective of a further education college
is shown below with some of its associated projects.

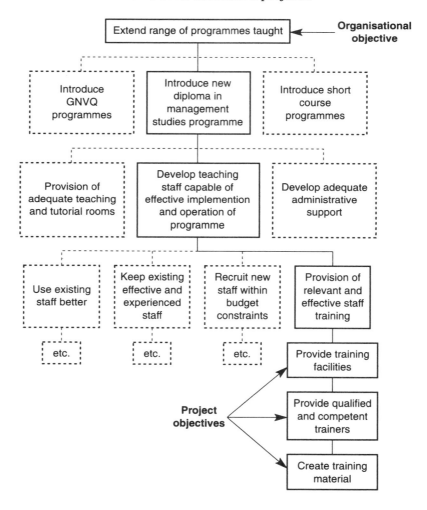

Objectives hierarchy

Another way of ensuring this compatibility is to use project objective
check lists. These provide, for the project creator, a way of checking
out the project against the goals the organisation has set for itself.

Their content and detail will, of course, reflect both the nature and direction of the organisational objectives. For example, the project check list for an organisation whose overriding objective is to achieve enhanced profitability will focus on issues such as:

- project payback period
- capital required
- project rate of return
- financial risk involved
- project net present value.

A project objectives check list for another organisation that is looking at the alternatives for replacement of its well proven but obsolete production process may be concerned with such issues as:

- technical risk involved in a new process
- impact on product quality
- effect on organisation image
- market and product quality implications of keeping the existing process going.

29

Not all of your projects will be about replacing old with new, and some of them will be concerned with the enhancement or improvement of existing features of your workplace. As we saw in Chapter 1 these features can be concerned with attitudes, morale, motivation or even organisational structure. The project objectives check lists for these projects and their 'cousins', which are concerned with enhancing or improving the physical aspects of our working environments, will share much in common with those illustrated above, but will also focus on issues such as:

- a project's contribution to an organisation's continuous performance improvement programme
- the contribution to or compatibility with other organisation-wide programmes such as Total Quality Management, BS 5750 Registration or Customer Charters.

Whichever method is used, the objectives of these projects, if they are to avoid rejection and achieve success, must be compatible with the main aims of the organisation and those of other projects.

Choosing the project

Choosing which project to implement requires a conscious formal decision, the consequences of which often involve capital expenditure and risk. This decision is often taken by a senior manager or a group of senior managers. In large organisations these groups are often called 'capital investment committees' because of their role in controlling and allocating the often scarce or limited capital required by the projects. In smaller organisations or within the departments of large organisations the choice may be made by individuals such as the company owner, the organisation's general manager or a head of department. The availability of the capital required to support these projects will be influenced significantly by a very wide range of variable factors such as interest rates, profit levels or market volatility, some of which are external to the organisation and hence beyond its control. This complexity is added to by the fact that while some of the competing projects are the results of organisational strategic decisions, others have not been anticipated and may owe their existence to events beyond the control of the organisation. As a result the availability of capital can range from the extreme of a fixed amount – with the consequence of what is termed 'capital rationing' – to the other extreme of unlimited funds where all projects are funded providing their marginal cost equals their marginal return. Almost always, however, the decision takers are faced with a demand for capital which exceeds that available and have to choose which projects are to be implemented. This choice can be undertaken in a number of different ways, which we will now look at. However that choice is made, it must ensure that the projects to be implemented:

- contribute to the well-being and survival of the organisation
- do not involve excessive foreseeable risks
- have objectives which are compatible with those of the organisation.

Choosing without numbers

Situations can occur in which projects arise without supporting clusters or clumps of information. This might happen, for example, when we need to react quickly to circumstances or when the information is not available or would cost too much to generate. When this occurs we still need to evaluate the project, but, from necessity, can only do so on a subjective rather that an objective basis. Examples of how and why this is done are as follows.

The operational crisis

This type of project often occurs as we become aware of an oncoming storm, flood, earthquake or hurricane. We may, for example, need to buy board to protect our shop windows from being blown in or build a protective dike to prevent our factory from flooding. Failure to do so may mean that we lose the ability to sell goods or manufacture our products. Under these circumstances formal project evaluation is not only impractical but also irrelevant. If, despite these preventative measures, damage does occur to the office, factory or warehouse, then we may face a similar situation – we need to repair that damage if we are to stay in business. Again the use of formal project evaluation is not possible, credible or relevant. The focus of the management of these types of project shifts from estimating their costs and returns to controlling the required expenditure. The only exception to both of these circumstances happens when the cost of prevention or repair exceeds the value of the shop or factory.

Legal requirement

The laws, statutory rules and regulations that tell us what we can and cannot do in our organisations are often the subject of change or reinterpretation. As a consequence the ways in which we operate our offices, factories and warehouses may also have to change. While we may be able to estimate the costs of projects generated by these changes, we have no choice about their implementation. Again the focus of the management of this type of project shifts from estimating the costs and returns to that of controlling the required expenditure. Examples might include the treatment of fume or effluent or the provision of access for disabled employees.

Employee welfare projects

This type of project is generally concerned with the provision or improvement of facilities such as staff canteens, restaurants, sports facilities and car parks. These projects can involve high levels of capital expenditure and, as such, require careful management. However, while they often reflect organisation policy, they rarely, if ever, generate direct financial returns.

Organisational status or power projects

All managers possess organisational power, and some managers need to exert that power by influencing the selection of a 'favourite' project. The motives for this are varied. In large organisations a manager's stay in any one post or role is often limited and the performance in that role will influence his or her selection for more senior positions. One result of this can be a tendency to favour projects with a rapid effect on annual profit, often at the expense of long term, slow growth strategic projects. Other examples of this influence, which can often bypass the formal project selection procedures, may reflect the intuition or 'gut feel' of experienced, capable and powerful managers or the idiosyncrasies of powerful individuals.

Competitive advantage

In the fiercely competitive and often volatile business environment of the 1990s, an organisation's ability to maintain a competitive advantage over its rivals can make a significant contribution to its profitability. Under these circumstances an organisation may sanction a project without the normal project evaluation procedures, thus saving time, entering the marketplace first and lessening the risk of information 'leakage' to its rivals.

Ranking

This is one of the techniques often used to order a group of similar projects. It is based upon the ranking, relative to each other, of these projects under a number of headings. The project with the best total ranking is then chosen for implementation. The headings selected will reflect the nature of the projects but must be equally applicable to all projects. For example, the choice between the different sorts of vehicle needed to answer a small company's product delivery needs might have headings which reflect capital cost, maintenance cost, insurance cost, ease of parking, load bearing capacity, ease of loading and unloading and fuel costs. The subsequent ranking matrix might be as shown in the table opposite, in which ranking 1 is best and 3 is worst. In this case alternative A would be selected despite its high maintenance cost and difficulty in load access.

Heading	Alternative		
	A	B	C
Capital cost	1	2	3
Maintenance cost	3	1	2
Insurance cost	2	3	1
Ease of parking	1	3	2
Load capacity	1	2	3
Ease of loading and unloading	3	1	2
Fuel costs	1	3	2
Total	12	15	15

The ranking process

This type of ranking process:

- can be easily applied
- requires 'better or worse than' data rather than absolute data
- can be undertaken quickly.

The ranking process can be further enhanced by the use of weighting factors that can reflect the relative importance of the individual headings.

Choosing with numbers

For most projects, the nature and size of their consequences and risks mean that they need to be evaluated with more care and precision. This is done by the use of methods based on numerical data. The following are examples of how and why this can be done.

Payback

The payback method of evaluating projects works out how long it will take for the project to pay back its initial capital cost. For example, a project which cost £10,000 to implement may have an annual profit of £2,500. The payback period for this project will be:

$$\frac{\text{Implementation cost}}{\text{Annual profit}} = \frac{£10,000}{£2,500} = 4 \text{ years}$$

When comparing projects, the project with the shortest payback period will be the one chosen. While this method is simple and easy to use it does have some significant limitations. It assumes, for example, that:

■ cash flows after the payback period are of no interest despite the fact that if equipment is involved it will have scrap values and may also have increasing operating or maintenance costs towards the end of its life

■ money does not change in value as time passes.

It can, however, be used to evaluate and compare low cost projects for which the complications of more sophisticated methods are unnecessary.

Rate of return

The rate of return for a project is found by dividing the annual profit by the implementation cost. For our earlier project this gives a rate of return of:

$$\frac{\text{Annual profit}}{\text{Implementation cost}} \times 100 = \frac{2,500}{10,000} \times 100 = 25\%$$

When this method is used to compare a number of projects, the project with the highest rate of return will be the one chosen. While this method is simple and easy to use it too has some significant limitations. For example, it:

■ assumes that the value of money does not change with time
■ calculates an average rate of return for the period considered
■ can, unless the period considered is extended to include the end of the equipment life span, ignore the fact that equipment will have scrap values and may have increasing operating or maintenance costs towards the end of its life.

The latter of these can be overcome by using methods of estimating the change in equipment value and then recalculating capital values and returns for each year. However, the fact that this method ignores the change in money value with time means that its use, like payback periods, is limited to low cost projects for which the complications of more sophisticated methods are unnecessary.

ઈ Pause for reflection ઈ

In the autumn of 1923 the price of goods in Germany was increasing by 30,000% per month.

Net present value

This method of evaluating projects ignores factors like the changing values of goods and equipment and concentrates on making allowance for the fact that the value of money changes with time. It does so by converting all of the future earnings of a project to their present value.

The following equation is used:

$$\text{Present value} = \frac{\text{Future value}}{(1 + r)^n}$$

where n = number of years
and r = assumed interest rate
or cost of capital

This means that, with an assumed interest rate of 10 per cent, a project with an implementation cost of £400 and projected profit pattern as follows:

Year number	1	2	3	4
Annual profit (£)	120	150	140	160

will have a net present value as follows:

Year number	0	1	2	3	4
Annual profit (£)	−400	$\dfrac{120}{(1+0.1)^1}$	$\dfrac{150}{(1+0.1)^2}$	$\dfrac{140}{(1+0.1)^3}$	$\dfrac{160}{(1+0.1)^4}$

109.10 ◄
123.97 ◄
105.20 ◄

Total present value   109.30 ◄
= 447.57

Net present value = 447.57 − 400 = 47.57

This process brings all the projected future cash flows to their values at the decision date. If the sum of these discounted future cash flows is greater than the implementation cost, then the value of the organisation will increase and the project is worthwhile. The greater the difference, the more worthwhile is the project. If the value of the sum of these discounted future cash flows is less than the implementation cost, then the project lessens the value of the organisation and should not be implemented.

Profitability index

The ratio of the sum of the net present values to capital required for implementation is sometimes called the profitability index. For a project to be accepted its value must exceed one, and the higher the value the more chance the project has of being chosen. For our previous example the profitability index would have been:

$$\frac{447.57}{400} = 1.119$$

Internal rate of return

This method of project evaluation uses the calculation methods applied in the net present value technique to make allowance for the fact that the value of money does change with time, but focuses on the percentage return generated by the project rather than its net present value. It does this by calculating the net present worth values for a project at various levels of interest and plots these on a graph (see below).

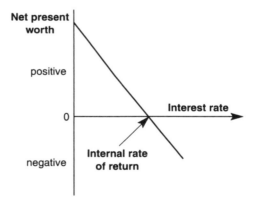

The internal rate of return

The interest rate at which the curve gives zero net present worth is called the internal rate of return, and the higher this figure is, the better the project. The choice of whether to implement a project is based on the value of this internal rate of return. If this exceeds the cost to the organisation of borrowing capital, then the project is acceptable. If it is below this cost, then the project will be rejected.

36

Sensitivity analysis and simulation

Both of these techniques seek to find out what will happen to the net positive value of a project if the assumptions made in calculating that value change. These complex techniques are generally used on high risk or very high implementation cost projects and use sophisticated mathematical techniques.

Summary

- *Selection of the 'right' project is a key first step in the management of a successful project.*

- *All projects involve risk and uncertainty.*

- *Risk and uncertainty cannot be eliminated but can be reduced by:*
  - *identifying the type, level and source of foreseeable risks*
  - *taking necessary steps (if possible) to reduce or eliminate those risks*
  - *deciding whether or not to accept those risks.*

- *The chosen project will:*
  - *contribute to the health of the organisation*
  - *have objectives which are compatible with the organisation's objectives and other organisational projects.*

- *Projects can be chosen by numerical or non-numerical methods.*

- *Projects can be chosen because of their:*
  - *ability to answer:*
    - *a. the demands of crises*
    - *b. legal requirements*
    - *c. employees' welfare needs*
    - *d. managers' power or status needs*
    - *e. the organisation's competitive needs*
  - *relative ranking*
  - *payback period*
  - *rate of return*
  - *net present value*
  - *internal rate of return.*

37

Organising your project

Overview

Successful projects are organised, structured and managed in ways which enable them to answer both effectively and efficiently the needs of those involved. This chapter looks at the ways in which projects can be organised and reviews the influence of a number of key factors on the nature of that organisation.

Objectives

By the end of this chapter you should have a better understanding of:
- **the conflicts between the needs of the client, the project and the project team**
- **organisations and their projects**
- **the ways in which projects can be organised**
- **the influence of such factors as:**
  - **the client organization**
  - **project duration**
  - **the nature of project outcomes**
- **the need for the project specification, role and responsibility definitions, budget and accounts, and change control procedure.**

Discord and conflict

As we saw in the previous chapter, successful projects:

- contribute to the well-being and survival of the client organisation
- do not involve excessive foreseeable risks
- have objectives which are compatible with the objectives of that organisation.

Successful projects also need to be organised, structured and managed in ways which answer the often conflicting needs of:

- the client organisation
- the project
- the project team.

The effects and influences of these conflicts are often potent and long-lasting and they can, unless resolved, place a considerable limit upon the success potential of any project. For example, the client will need to ensure that the project:

- gives value for money and a fair return on its implementation cost
- is completed as and when required.

In order to answer those needs the client may wish to have:

- considerable involvement in and influence over all project decisions – even those concerned with the fine detail of the project
- the freedom to change or modify the project objectives as and when required
- a project team which consists of people who owe allegiance to the client organisation.

But, in contrast to the above, the project team will wish to have:

- the continuing presence of a project manager who has clear and unconditional authority on all project issues
- members who are directly responsible only to that project manager
- the freedom to make decisions without the constraints of outside interference
- a clear identity which is separate from the client organisation.

The already evident conflict between these two sets of needs increases further when we look at the requirements of the project, which are that it should have objectives that are :

- clear
- unambiguous
- specific
- frozen or fixed at the earliest opportunity.

These project objectives should also be expressed in numerical terms:

- **time** (e.g. to start on 20 January 1996 and end by 13 December 1997)
- **money** (e.g. to be implemented at a total cost of £20,000)
- **performance** (e.g. to produce a 200 page soft-back book with line diagrams)

39

■ **quality** (e.g. a book designed to meet the needs of middle managers).

A further and obvious need is that sufficient resources of money, equipment and skilled people should be available to the project to ensure that the above objectives can be met.

There are very many circumstances in which these differing needs are in conflict with each other. For example, the client's need to modify and adapt the project to meet the changing and often volatile needs of the marketplace is often in conflict with the project's need to have its objective frozen at the earliest opportunity and the needs of the project team to be able to manage the project free from outside interference. The key to resolving these conflicts and creating the outcome of a successful project lies not only in the compromises negotiated (see Chapter 11) but also in the way in which the project is organised. However, before we look at the options for organising projects, we first need to look, albeit briefly, at the nature of the organisation itself.

40

Clubs, companies, conglomerates and countries

All of these are examples of that often complex and paradoxical entity which we call the organisation. They all have members and aims and, in one way or another, assign, set aside or earmark resources which enable them to direct their activities towards those aims. The basic organisation is often defined as being a 'systematic arrangement' of parts or elements which has a definite purpose, but it can also be seen as a voluntary gathering of people striving towards chosen objectives. The word 'organisation' is often used to describe many of the groups, clubs, establishments or societies in which we work or play and these can vary enormously in both size and complexity. They can, for example, be small – consisting of limited numbers of people with a common interest such as playing golf or chess – or they can be huge, complex and powerful – as with our governments or the conglomerates which provide so many of the goods and services which we consume. When we look at the formal structures of these organisations we find that these also show considerable variety. They can be, for example, hierarchical, with formally defined roles and levels of power, or almost organic in form, with very limited formality or hierarchy present. Some of the ways in which these structures can be depicted are shown opposite.

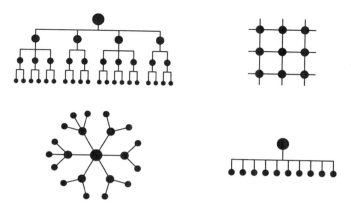

Organisational structures

These organisations abound in all our lives – they are everywhere and embrace every aspect of our existence. They sell us goods or services, educate our children, collect our rubbish, influence the political decisions made about the resources and services of our communities and countries, and provide us with money in exchange for our services and skills. They also provide resources for most of our projects and can often, in one form or another, be the clients for whom the projects are created and managed. And yet, despite all this variety and diversity, all organisations, when stripped down to their basic form, have two common characteristics:

■ they consist of collections of individuals who share a common purpose
■ they have or use systems which are both formal and informal.

These organisational systems are concerned with:

■ the 'politics' of power and influence
■ decisions about the allocation and use of resources such as materials, money and information
■ the duties and responsibilities of occupations, roles and jobs.

The commonalty of these characteristics means that all organisations have:

■ **leaders** – with varying levels of real or nominal power
■ **structures** – which can be rigid or flexible and are concerned with roles, responsibilities and occupations
■ **procedures** – which are concerned with the ways in which the objectives of the organisation are achieved.

41

However, even when we have these leaders, structures and procedures we still need the vital ingredient of people. People bring organisations to life – they can make them work despite their complexity, and without them the leader cannot lead and the structures and procedures will remain hollow, ineffective and impotent shells.

Projects and organisations

When we first compare projects and organisations we find that they appear to have much in common. They both have objectives, targets and goals as their desired outcomes and they both have people as a vital element. They also, as we shall see later in this book, both have leaders, structures, systems and procedures. However, when we probe further into these goal-centred mechanisms we will find that differences begin to emerge and these are vital to the ways in which the organisation and the project are organised and managed.

42

The first of these differences is concerned with the time-scale of their activities. Organisations are primarily concerned with the long run and with long term targets. Their prime objective is that of survival, of continued existence, and in order to achieve this they are often prepared to sacrifice their original aims or radically alter their form or structure. This survival is not a time related goal but a continual one that runs in front of the organisation like a standing wave on the bow of a ship. Nevertheless, organisations do manage, co-ordinate and control the detail of their short and medium term activities. This, however, is only undertaken as a way of ensuring or attempting to ensure that the organisation will reach that goal of continuing survival.

&a Pause for reflection a&

'Organisations exist to achieve purposes that individuals cannot achieve on their own.'
Professor Rosemary Stewart

In contrast, projects are ephemeral in nature. Despite the often solid and considerable nature of their outcomes, all projects are like the dragonflies of summer – here for a short while and then gone. Projects exist only for a short time span, in relation to that of an organisation, and their objectives are time specific – they must be achieved by a date or time which is known at the project's birth. Once these objectives are achieved then the projects will voluntarily terminate their activities.

As we probe further we find that not only has the question as to what is the best structure for an organisation been the subject of considerable debate and discussion but that there are also many different views about its form and nature. These range from the massive and rigid monoliths of bureaucracy to organisational forms which are much more fluid and responsive. In comparison, project organisation has been the subject of only limited debate and, as a result, the ways in which projects are organised is often the result of limited thought or discussion. 'We have always done it this way' is often the cry when the who, how and what of project organisations are decided. Finally, our probing the differences between projects and organisations reminds us that, as we saw in Chapter 2, while projects are concerned with unique, one-off outcomes, organisations are involved in replication, repetition and hybridisation of their outcomes.

When we stand back and look at these differences what we see is: 43

	Organisations	*Projects*
Time horizon	Long term and continual	Short/medium term, defined and limited
Objectives	Continuing survival	Completion and termination
Outcomes	Replicas or hybrids	Unique and one-off

Not only does this comparison strengthen the view that projects are a tool which managers can use in pursuit of the organisation's objectives but it also tells us where, in the wide spectrum of organisational activities, those projects can be applied. The powerful and flexible tool of the project is used to support the organizational activities of managing, co-ordinating and controlling its short and medium term activities in support of the goal of continuing survival. Projects are used to create the change that is often required to enable those activities to be conducted in a more efficient and more effective manner. They can also be used to redirect or even restructure the organisation towards the goal of survival.

Organising projects – the overview

Before we look at the detail of how projects can be organised it is worth reminding ourselves that all projects:

- have unique outcomes
- are concerned with change
- take place over a limited period of time
- use a variety of transitory resources.

It is also worth reminding ourselves that if these projects are to be managed successfully then they need to be organised, structured and managed in ways which answer the needs of:

- the client organisation
- the project
- the project team.

But, as we saw earlier, these needs are often in conflict with each other. Any project organisation must be not only robust enough to cope with those conflicts but also responsive enough to bring about those practical and pragmatic compromises, between these conflicting needs, that will ultimately ensure the success of the project.

44

The nature of the project organisation is also influenced by a number of other factors, which range from the client organisation's previous experience of projects and their management through to the detailed nature of the project itself. Key features among these are the project's:

- **duration** – as in days or decades
- **magnitude of cost** – as in hundreds or billions of pounds
- **complexity** – as in 20 or 35,000 interconnected activities
- **importance to the client** – as in 'vital to our survival' or 'just another project'
- **importance to the project team** – as in 'we are the best' or 'done this all before'
- **innovative nature** – as in ' Rocket to Mars' or 'yet another new magazine'.

Organising projects – the choices

We can begin to explore the choices available to us when we organise our projects by looking at two very different projects in the same organisation. The first of these is a low cost and short duration hospital project which is concerned with the transfer of a manual system for recording patient details that has proved effective in a small children's clinic to a small clinic for adults. The innovative level of this record system is low because its effectiveness and efficiency had been proved already, but it has not been used in the adult clinic and will be, to the people who work there, a new system. These same people will need that project to be successful as will the manager who chose the system. All of these factors lead to the conclusion that the organisation of this project is one which should be strongly influenced by the needs of the client. As such, that project organisation is likely to have:

■ a structure which reflects that of the client or adult clinic organisation
■ a full time project leader drawn from the staff of the adult clinic
■ part-time team members drawn from the staff of both clinics.

It will also be integrated into the existing organisation management and control systems. Such a project organisation will enable the adult clinic to draw on the experience gained by the staff of the children's clinic when starting up and operating the new system. It will also ensure that the staff of the adult clinic are involved in and respons-ible for the effective transfer and start-up of the system. In comparison, a project which is high cost, has a long time span and is concerned with the implementation of new technology or systems, such as the introduction of a complex, integrated, computer-driven management information system (MIS) for the whole of that same hospital, is likely to have different needs. These are reflected in a project organisation which has:

■ a project team separate from the hospital organisation
■ its own management and control systems
■ a structure related to the needs of the project rather than mirroring the structure of the client organisation.

Such a project organisation will enable the project to be managed efficiently and effectively. The measure of this achievement will be, as with all projects, the completion of the project to its planned duration, cost, performance and quality. A project of this size and complexity will demand:

■ high levels of skill in planning and managing large projects
■ strong and independent project management.

And these will need to be supported by:

■ knowledge and experience of MIS systems
■ experience of creating and introducing MIS systems.

These glimpses of two very different projects have shown us two of the ways in which projects can be organised. The first project, which

45

was concerned with the transfer of a manual client record system, had an organisation that was focused on answering the needs of the client. The second project, which was concerned with the creation of a hospital-wide MIS, had an organisation that was focused on the needs of the project. Some of the differences between the client focus and the project focus can be seen below.

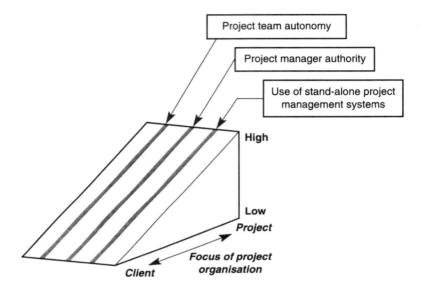

Client and project focus

Organising projects – the detail

There are three main types of project organisation:

- client focused organisation
- matrix organisation
- project focused organisation.

In order to make sure that you choose the 'right' organisation for your project we need to look at the pros and cons of each of these types of project organisation.

The client focused organisation

This type of project organisation integrates the project into the existing structure of the client organisation. This usually means that the project is staffed by people who work for the client organisation and can also mean that it is staffed only on a part-time basis. However, the use of this type of project organisation does mean that the project can tap into and use the functional skills and experience of the organisation and ensures that key experts are used by both the project and the organisation. Its other advantages include:

- compatibility of project and organisation procedures and systems
- compatibility of project and organisation objectives.

However, this type of project organisation does have its disadvantages, such as:

- the day to day needs of the organisation often dominate resources allocation decisions
- the project has a reduced ability to induce change, particularly where it is concerned with changing attitudes, norms or standards
- client-project contact is often indirect
- project team allegiances are to their functional 'home' – not the project
- the authority of the project manager is limited.

The location of the project within the client organisation will depend upon the nature of the project outcomes. For example, a project with a strong production 'flavour' is placed under the supervision of the Production Department and a project which aims to change quality standards and procedures will find a home in the Quality Department.

Project focused organisation

In this type of project organisation the project team exists as a self-contained unit with its own resources, staff, premises, etc. This team is separate from the rest of the organisation and communicates with it by means of progress reports which are usually delivered at regular intervals – monthly or two-weekly, for example – but can also occur after or before crucial project activities. Much of this communication will take place via a senior management position which is high enough in the client organisation to eliminate functional bias or conflict. The advantages of the project focused organisation include:

- the team has a strong identity and members are committed to the project
- the team is managed by a project manager who has full control over the project

47

- communication is direct
- decision taking and problem solving can be swift.

Disadvantages include:

- duplication of staff if several projects are in progress
- incompatibilities can develop between project and organisation procedures, systems and objectives
- loss of skill and experience of project team members at project end.

An example of this type of project organisation is shown below.

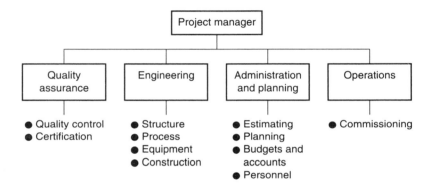

The project focus organisation

Matrix project organisation

This is usually seen as a compromise – a middle position – between the extremes of the project focused and the client focused organisations. In its simplest form, the project manager draws the people resources required from each of the client organisation's functional departments as shown opposite.

The advantages of this type of project organisation include:

- its ability to draw on client organisation resources as and when required
- the compatibility between project and organisation procedures, systems and objectives.

The disadvantages of the matrix type of project organisation include:

- team members have two bosses – a functional boss and a project boss

```
                              CEO
                               |
        ┌──────────────┬───────┴───────┬──────────────┐
   Marketing       Accounts        R and D        Personnel
   and sales
       |               |               |               |
Project───(1)────────(2)────────────(1.5)───────────(4)
manager
```

Number of people assigned
from department

The matrix organisation

- the balance of power, between the client organisation and the project manager, is often delicate
- the project manager takes project administrative decisions and the organisation's functional managers take project technical decisions.

This form of project management has been seen, in the past, as an effective and efficient way to manage organisational projects. However, its popularity has declined for reasons which include its considerable potential to degenerate into disorganised chaos and the fact that its team members find considerable difficulty in working for two bosses.

Selecting your project organisation

Choosing the 'right' organisation for your project can make a big difference to the way in which that project is managed and even to its ultimate acceptance by the client organisation. Despite what other books on project management might tell you, there are no 'golden rules' – it is, as with many management decisions, a question of drawing from your own experience and exercising your judgement. This judgement will be about what type of organisation will be compatible with the client organisation and the experience will be about what sort of project organisations have and have not worked before. The judgement must also take in account what you already know about the project – its outcomes, risks, costs and duration – together with any special technology or knowledge that is required or involved. A practical and effective way of bringing together that information and providing a framework in which you can exercise your judgement about what type of project organisation is right for your project is shown below.

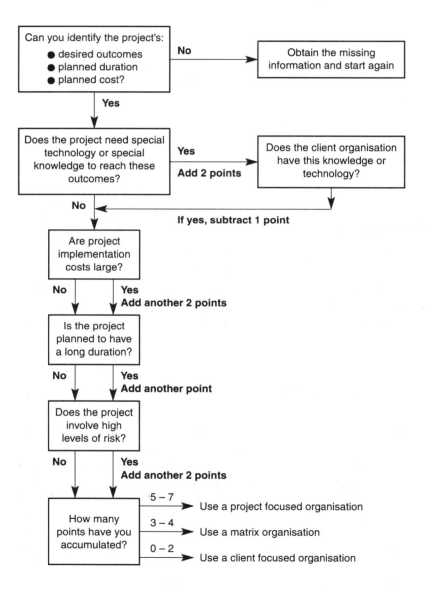

Choosing your project organisation

Organising your project

Once you have chosen the type of project organisation which you feel is right for your project the next step is to begin the process of organising the project. This is a complex and demanding task which will draw on many of the skills that you have developed as a manager of routine day to day activities. Later chapters of this book will look in detail at how you can apply those skills to the processes of planning (Chapter 5) and managing (Chapter 6) the project, as well as monitoring and controlling its progress (Chapter 12) and building the project team (Chapter 7). Nevertheless, despite the wealth of information contained in these and other chapters we must at this early stage in our journey begin to lay the foundations of our future success. We shall do that by looking at the core materials that we need to get together in order to begin our journey to a successful project.

51

Project specification

This has the primary purpose of:

■ providing a description of the project
■ defining its objectives.

It can consist, for a low cost, limited duration project, of a single sheet of paper or, for a complex, high cost, long duration project, of a folder with a number of sections and appendices. Whatever the size and structure of this specification its roots lie as far back as the time when the project was 'just a gleam in the client's eye' and it will have been modified and amended as the project developed. However, once the project and its implementation costs have been approved, the specification should then be subject to very little change. It should become the source of definitive information about the project's:

■ goals and objectives
■ scope
■ organisation
■ budget
■ justification.

Use the check list overleaf to check out your project specification.

PROJECT SPECIFICATION CHECK LIST

Does the project specification state:
- what the project has undertaken to supply?   Yes ☐ No ☐
- when it is to be supplied by?   Yes ☐ No ☐
- where it is to be supplied?   Yes ☐ No ☐
- at what cost ?   Yes ☐ No ☐

Does it also state:
- what project team roles are to be carried out?   Yes ☐ No ☐
- what the responsibilities of these roles are?   Yes ☐ No ☐
- who has been appointed to those roles?   Yes ☐ No ☐

Does it tell you:
- what tools and techniques will be used to plan and
  control the project?   Yes ☐ No ☐
- what sums have been initially estimated for
  what use?   Yes ☐ No ☐
- how and when client communication will take place? Yes ☐ No ☐

Key: If you have more than two no's then you need to review and change your project specification – before you have a problem!

52

Project roles and responsibilities

Clear, well defined role and responsibility definitions are essential to the successful operation of all project organisations. They should be generated for all members of the project team and should define:

- what the role's objectives are
- how you will measure the success of the role
- what the role involves
- to whom the role reports
- what authority the role has
- what involvement the role has in client communications such as meetings or reports.

A well written role and responsibility definition should not exceed two sides of A4 paper – any more than that indicates you are unsure about the nature and extent of the role's definition and responsibilities.

Project accounts and budgets

As we will see in more detail in Chapter 8, project accounts and budgets have different functions and purposes. However, at this time we need to note that they are both important and, far from being number crunching 'exercises', can both make a considerable contribution to the success of your project. At this early stage in your project, it is, therefore, important that you define:

- a firm budget figure for the project
- procedures for approvals and payments.

Project change control

A change is a departure from something previously agreed or established, and for a project this may involve departures from agreed:

- plans
- specifications
- briefs
- contracts.

All of these and other changes will have implications for the project's:

- duration
- cost
- outcome
- quality.

Despite all your efforts to prevent change, it will still occur. Changes can come about because they:

- are necessary (mistakes, changes in legislation, etc.)
- represent improvements (new technology, better design, etc.)

It is vital to the success of the project that, at the earliest possible opportunity, the following are defined or established:

- a clear, accessible and unambiguous statement of the project's 'base' line as, for example, will be contained in the project specification mentioned above
- effective procedures for the definition, evaluation and approval of proposed changes to that specification.

Failure to achieve these actions will result in a 'runaway' project which is out of control and for which the final outcome, duration, quality and costs bear little resemblance to those contained in the original approved specification. Overleaf is an example of a basic project change control form.

PROJECT CHANGE REQUEST	
Number:	Date:
Approved /Rejected / Held	
Proposed change	
Reason for change	
Areas affected Documents and drawings affected	
Requested by: _____	Evaluated by: _____ Date:

Project change control form

54

Summary

■ Selection of the 'right' project organisation is a key step towards a successful project.

■ That organisation will balance the conflicting needs of:
  – the client organisation
  – the project team
  – the project.

■ The main types of project organisation are:
  – client focused organisation
  – matrix organisation
  – project organisation.

■ Choosing which of these is right for your project involves:
  – judgement
  – knowledge of what has worked in the past
  – a good understanding of the nature of the project outcomes, risks, costs, duration and special technology or knowledge needs.

■ The first and essential steps in organising your project involve the generation of the project:
  – specification
  – roles and responsibility definitions
  – budget and accounting procedures
  – change control procedures.

Planning your project

> *Overview*
>
> **Planning is a powerful and effective contributor to the success of a project. In this chapter we look at the tools that enable the project's use of time and physical resources to be planned to maximum effect.**
>
> *Objectives*
>
> **By the end of this chapter you should have a better understanding of:**
> - **the steps and stages of the planning process**
> - **planning tools such as**
>   - **– Gantt charts**
>   - **– Activity on Arrow networks**
>   - **– Activity on Node networks**
> - **the planning of physical resources**
> - **the use of computers for project planning.**

Planning – why bother?

In this, the last decade of the twentieth century, planning appears to have become a dirty word. In our workplaces, adaptability, responsiveness to customer needs, employee empowerment, quality circles, decentralisation and sweeping organisational re-engineering are all symptoms of a climate which has transformed the winds of change of the 1960s into the hurricanes of disorder and chaos of the 1990s. These and many other changes have challenged and overthrown many traditional management wisdoms that were built on the concepts of planning and control.

But is planning an outmoded and outdated concept or is it a powerful and flexible tool whose use managers have to relearn in the volatile 1990s? Successful projects require planning – they don't just happen – and that planning must be capable of withstanding the buffeting of the increasingly unsettled environment in which we all work.

Planning is the act of creating a plan, and a typical dictionary tells us that this is a diagram, table or programme which indicates the relationships of a set of objects or the times, places, etc. of intended actions. For most of us, our plans are about actions and, if they are to contribute to the success of those actions, they tell us:

- when they are to be done
- who is to do them
- what equipment, tools, etc. we need to do them.

However, plans are not just detailed lists of actions. At their worst they can represent the rigid, inflexible and doctrinaire demands of others which suppress and choke our creativity and spontaneity. But at their best they are powerful tools which embody our visions, hopes and desires. These plans can be used flexibly to communicate the why, what, how and when of those visions and hopes to others and form the basis of those co-operative efforts that, as we will see in Chapter 7, characterise successful teams. But, whatever the management theorists might have in store for us next, we will all continue to need to reach out and try to shape and control our futures. Plans are a proven and effective tool which, if used well, will enable us to do just that.

57

Planning and projects

A project plan is the mechanism by which we convert the objectives of a project from statements of intent to the concrete reality of achieved outcomes. If we fail to create such a plan then not only do we put at risk our ability to create the desired outcome of the project but we also limit our ability to create that outcome at the desired:

- cost
- time
- quality.

We saw in Chapter 4 that in creating the project specification we provided a source of information which told us, among other things, what are the project's goals and objectives. This definition provides us with our starting point for the creation of the project plan. But in order to convert those goals and objectives into a plan we also need to know the answers to such questions as:

- what actions are needed?
- when do these actions need to start or finish?

- how long they will take?
- who will do them?
- what equipment, tools and materials are needed?

Typical answers to these questions, for a small project which is familiar to many of us, are given in the following example.

Project goals and objectives: to redecorate a small bedroom

Actions needed:
- remove furniture, curtains and light shades
- protect carpet
- strip off old wallpaper and remove waste
- fill major pits and other defects in walls and sand down
- remove old paint from woodwork and remove waste
- repair defects and sand down woodwork
- dust/vacuum to remove dust
- wash down ceiling
- paint ceiling
- prime, undercoat and topcoat paint woodwork
- paper walls
- clean up waste and remove carpet protection
- replace light shades, furniture and curtains.

Completion by: 10 December

Duration: four days (two weekends)

Actions by: Philip and Linda Baguley

Equipment, tools and material needed:

Paint brushes	Paint roller
Paint remover and scrapers	Wallpaper scrapers
Filler	Sandpaper
Step ladder	Wallpaper adhesive and brush
Pasting table	Scissors, measure, plumb line
Plastic sheets	Emulsion paint for ceiling
Primer, undercoat and	Wallpaper brush
gloss paint for woodwork	Vacuum cleaner
Wallpaper	
Duster	
Bucket, cloths and detergent.	

We also need to know what the budgeted cost of the project is and in what way the quality of the outcome is to be defined since both of these could affect either the way that we undertake the required actions or even the actions themselves. For example, in the bedroom redecoration project illustrated a limited budget would influence what quality of wallpaper we buy and might even persuade us to paint over the existing wood finish, thus eliminating the cost of the primer, undercoat, paint remover and scrapers. All of these cost based decisions have, as we saw in Chapter 2, implications for the other dimensions of the specification:

- outcome performance – i.e. durability of wallpaper and paintwork
- time to completion – i.e. less time needed
- outcome quality or fitness for purpose – i.e. does it look good?

We also need to know if any of these actions cannot be started before other actions are finished. In the jargon of project planning this is usually called 'interdependency' and when we look at our bedroom redecoration project, we find that:

Action	Can only be completed after action no.
1 Remove furniture, curtains and light shades	–
2 Protect carpet	1
3 Strip off old wallpaper and remove waste	2
4 Fill major pits and other defects in walls and sand down	3
5 Remove old paint from woodwork and remove waste	2
6 Repair defects and sand down woodwork	5
7 Dust/vacuum to remove dust	4 and 6
8 Wash down ceiling	2
9 Paint ceiling	8
10 Prime, undercoat and topcoat paint woodwork	5 and 7
11 Paper walls	4, 9 and 10
12 Clean up waste and remove carpet protection	11
13 Replace light shades, furniture and curtains	12

When we look at the list of these activities and their interdependencies we begin to get some sense of how the project might be planned and questions start to emerge such as 'can we strip the old wallpaper and the old paint at the same time?' or 'can we sand down the woodwork and wash down the ceiling at the same time?' . Before we can answer these questions we need to know how long each of these activities will take. The process of estimating activity durations is often described as a mixture of science, experience and intuition. It is, however, an important contributor to the credibility and usability of the project plan. Estimates can be made by using information, for example, from paint manufacturers ('A drying time of two hours is normal'), people who have done it before (friends, family or book authors) and your own experience (what did we do last time?). At this stage it is not necessary to have estimates which are absolutely accurate. For our bedroom redecoration project it will be adequate to estimate to the nearest half an hour, while on larger and longer projects estimates with an accuracy of ± half a day will be adequate at this stage in the planning process.

60

Whatever the accuracy level of our initial estimate, a successful project needs a plan which meets the following standards:

- **Content.** The plan should contain enough detail to make it meaningful and usable but not so much detail that it becomes unnecessarily complicated. That content should also be clear and unambiguous.
- **Understandability.** A plan which can be easily understood by all who use it is vital to the success of the project.
- **Changeability.** An effective plan is one which can be easily changed, updated and revised.
- **Usability.** The plan must be in a form which means that it can be easily used to monitor project progress and as means of communication.

A good plan will have all the above characteristics but will still need the skills, abilities and creativity of people to make it come to life. A bad plan will not only be difficult to understand or contain inadequate or irrelevant detail but it will also limit or even neutralise the vital contribution of those people's skills, abilities and creativity.

❧ *Pause for reflection* ❧
'It is a bad plan that admits no modification.'
Publilius Syrus, 1st century BC

Bars and charts

One of the oldest and simplest forms of the project plan is the bar chart or Gantt chart. This was developed in the second decade of the twentieth century by an American engineer called Henry L. Gantt who was a follower of F.W. Taylor's school of so-called 'Scientific Management'. Despite its age, the bar or Gantt chart remains a popular and useful method of presenting information about the project plan. It has:

- a horizontal time-scale
- a vertical list of activities
- a horizontal line or bar for each activity
- lines or bars of a length proportional to the time needed to complete the activity.

Below is a typical Gantt chart.

Time / Activity	Hours					
	1	2	3	4	5	6
A						
B						
C						
D						

The Gantt chart

In this example, activities A, B, C and D are to be started and completed one after each other and have durations of 1.5, 1.5, 1 and 1.5 hours respectively. As well as providing planning information the chart can also be used to monitor progress. In the above example, if everything has been completed to schedule, the chart will, after 3 hours of elapsed time, look like the version overleaf.

In all projects there are activities which are carried out in parallel with each other or at the same time, and these can be easily shown on the Gantt chart as the second diagram overleaf shows. Another feature which is crucial to the management of all projects is the project 'critical path'. This represents the sequence of activities which leads to the shortest project completion time and which, if delayed, will hold up the completion of the project. This path and the sequence of activities that

Time / Activity	Hours					
	1	2	3	4	5	6
A	▓▓▓▓▓					
B			▓▓▓▓			
C					▭	
D						▭

Gantt chart used for monitoring

makes it up tells us which of all the project activities we need to focus our attention on in order to ensure project completion on time. Both the critical path and 'same time' or parallel activities are shown below:

Time / Activity	Hours					
	1	2	3	4	5	6
A	▭					
B		▭			Critical path	
C	Parallel	▭				
D	activities	▭				
E				▭		

Parallel activities and critical path

The Gantt chart, with its time-scale base and visual representation of activity duration and completion, gives us a clear and easily understood picture of the project. This chart requires limited training for its creation and use and can be drawn by hand on standard graph paper or paper with pre-printed columns. There are also several proprietary versions of the wall mounted Gantt chart, with magnetic or special 'click in' strips that can be used to display plans for projects involving as many as 100 activities.

Despite the introduction of sophisticated network project planning systems, the Gantt chart remains one of the most popular forms of project plan. It does, however, have its limitations. The updating or revision of a large, manually generated Gantt chart can be an arduous and time consuming task which often occurs at a time when the updated or revised plan is urgently needed. While this can be bypassed using computer generated Gantt charts, the next drawback is not so easily overcome. This limitation is that the Gantt chart cannot easily or clearly show activity interdependencies. These, as we saw earlier, occur when one activity cannot start until another preceding activity has finished, and we need to know about them if we are to manage our project effectively and efficiently. For both of these reasons, Gantt charts are not easy to use on large or complex projects or with projects for which the plan changes frequently because of high levels of uncertainty about activity completion times. However, the Gantt chart does have significant advantages and is often used:

- **on small projects** – as a planning system with low training demands and a direct visual image which is easily understood
- **on large projects** – in its computer generated form, in parallel with network systems as an aid to communication.

Networks

63

One way of overcoming the problems of the Gantt chart is to use network planning systems. These first became popular during the late 1950s and early uses included large and complex projects such as the development of the Polaris missile/submarine and the construction of large chemical plants. Since that time the use of networks for project planning has become widespread and, not surprisingly, a number of hybrid versions have been developed. These were designed primarily to enable the project plan to cope with high levels of uncertainty and complexity. Three examples of these sophisticated network planning systems are GERT (Graphical Evaluation and Review Technique), PERT (Programme Evaluation and Review Technique) and VERT (Venture Evaluation and Review Technique). We, however, will be focusing our attention on simpler versions of the network planning system and, in particular, looking at the two primary types of network plan. Both of these use structured networks to describe the sequence of the project activities and connections between those activities. They also:

- arrange these activities so that they flow from left to right
- use arrows to form the network
- locate squares or circles at the points of intersection or nodes of these arrows
- store information at these nodes.

However, they do use these arrows and nodes in very different ways as we can see below:

■ **activity on arrow or AOA networks** – These use an arrow to represent an activity and circles for the nodes which are the start and finish of that activity.

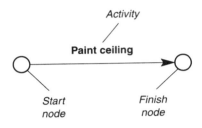

Activity on arrow example

■ **activity on node or AON networks** – These represent an activity by a box at the node and link activities together by using arrows.

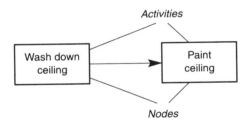

Activity on node example

Each of these types of network has different advantages and drawbacks and we shall now look at them in turn.

Activity on arrow networks

As we saw above the activity on arrow network is made up of arrows, which represent the project activities, and nodes, which represent the events of the beginning or end of these activities. An example of a simple network is shown in the diagram opposite in which:

■ the activities are identified by the letters a, b, c, d and e
■ the nodes are numbered 1, 2, 3, 4 and 5.

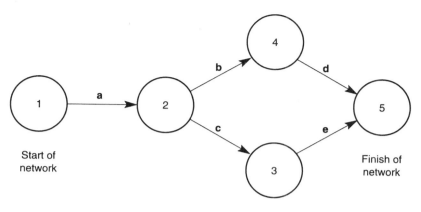

AOA network

When we take a closer look at this network, we see that:

■ the finish node of one activity is also the start node of the following activity – as we can see with activity b whose finish node (no. 4) is the start node for activity d

■ some of the activities take place at the same time – as we can see with activities b and c, which both start after activity a has been completed

■ several activities can start from one event, as when activities b and c start from event 2, or merge into one event, as when activities d and e merge into event 5.

But does this network tell us all that we want to know? The answer is no because, as it is currently drawn, the network does not have any information about:

■ how long the project or even any of the activities will take to complete

■ which sequence of activities leads to the shortest project completion time, i.e. which is the project critical path

■ whether any of the activities cannot be started before other actions are finished, i.e. whether any are interdependent.

In order to see how we can include this information into our activity on arrow project network we need to go back to the original data for these activities and see how we can use them to get the above information.

Activity	Duration (hr)	Can only be completed after activity
a	2	–
b	2.75	a
c	3.5	a
d	4	b and c
e	2	c

When we introduce this information what we find is that the network changes to the example given below.

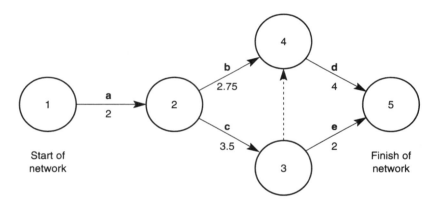

AOA network with activity durations

Here the dotted line (called a dummy activity) tells us that activity d cannot start until activities b *and* c are complete.

But this still does not give us all the facts and figures that we need, and in order to get to that point we have to calculate the rest of the information which is to be stored at the network nodes. This information will tell us:

- the **earliest time** that event can occur – the 'earliest event time' or EET
- the **latest time** that the event can occur – the 'latest event time' or LET.

These nodes will change to the example given opposite.

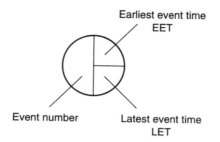

Earliest event time
EET

Event number   Latest event time
LET

AOA network node

The figures are calculated as follows:

- starting at the first event write the figure '0' in the EET location
- move to event no. 2, add the duration of activity a to the EET for event no. 1, giving an EET of 2, and write this in the EET location for event no. 2
- follow through the network adding each activity duration to the previous EET and writing the resultant figure into the EET location
- when you reach an event where two activities merge, as in no. 4, write in the highest figure generated for the EET. Note that dummy activities have a zero duration
- continue to the last event and write in the figure generated in both the EET and the LET locations
- starting at event no. 5, trace the network backwards, subtracting the duration of the following activity from the LET at each event and writing the figure generated in the LET location in the node at the event's start
- when you reach an event at which two activities merge (no. 2) write in the lowest LET calculated
- continue to the first event, at which you should have an LET which is the same as the EET for this event. If you haven't, then you've made a mistake – probably at an event where two or more activities merge.

The figures we have calculated give us a network which looks like the one illustrated overleaf.

Some of the arrows in this network are heavy and bold and these tell us which sequence of activities defines the overall project duration, i.e. the project critical path. We can also see that the project will take 9.5 hours to complete. But, if we look carefully we will also see that activity b, which starts after 2 hours of project duration, could

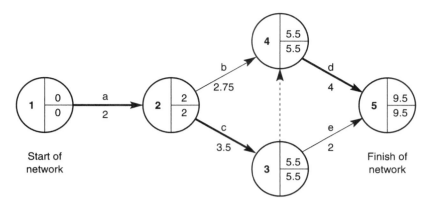

AOA network with more detail

finish at 2 + 2.75 = 4.75 hours but doesn't need to finish until activity c is completed, i.e. at 5.5 hours. Similarly, activity e could finish at 5.5 + 2 = 7.5 hours but need not finish until 9.5 hours. These differences between the time required and the time available for an activity are called the 'float' or 'slack' of that activity. This can be used by the project manager to:

■ delay the start of the activity as with activity e – we can delay its start until 9.5 – 2 = 7.5 hours
■ or, using the original start time, extend the duration of the activity by, for example, using fewer people or a different method, up to a maximum of 9.5 – 5.5 = 4 hours.

In the full AOA network this float is shown in the network nodes as given below.

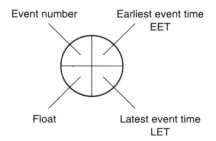

Full AOA network node

The resulting network, which has its critical path marked in bold lines, looks like the illustration opposite.

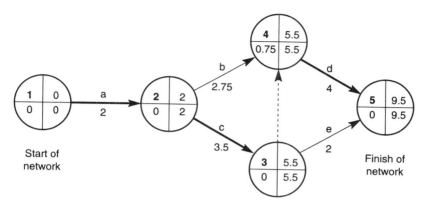

Full AOA network

As we noted earlier these AOA networks can be used under conditions of uncertainty to estimate probable project durations. To do so fully requires a detailed working knowledge of statistical theory, but approximations can be made by calculating what is called the 'expected activity duration' for each activity and using those to generate the network. This can be calculated by using the following equation:

$$\text{Expected activity duration} = \frac{(a + 4m + b)}{6}$$

where   a = estimated shortest activity duration
b = estimated longest activity duration
m = most likely activity duration.

Efficient and effective use of the AOA network requires both its creator and user to have considerable training and experience. It does, however, despite a lower visual impact than is gained from use of the Gantt chart, enable the project manager to:

■ work out the implications of activity duration changes, since the network does not require redrawing
■ examine the trade-offs between outcome, time, cost and quality.

In its computer driven form, the AOA network is often used to considerable effect on large and complex projects and it is, without doubt, the most popular form of project planning for this type of project. AOA networks can also be used, in the hand-written form, for small projects.

69

Activity on node networks

The activity on node or AON network uses, as we saw earlier, the nodes to represent the project activities and arrows to indicate their dependencies. This is demonstrated when we take the simple network that we used to illustrate AOA networks and convert it to an AON network as shown below.

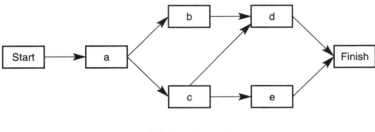

AON network

70

The activities are identified by the letters a, b, c, d and e, and are represented by squares; the dependencies, including the dummy, are represented by arrows. Note that the dotted line dummy activity of the AOA network has no equivalent in the AON network – activity d is merely shown to be dependent upon activities c and b. The squares at the nodes of the full AON network are structured as shown below:

Earliest start time	Latest start time
Activity description	
Activity duration	Float

AON node

The information carried in the node is generated in the same way as that for the AOA network, except that the backwards pass generates latest start times rather than latest event times. The resulting AON network is illustrated opposite, with, again, the critical path marked in bold lines.

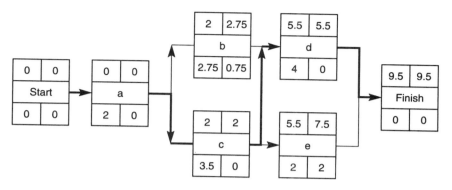

Detailed AON network

The advantages of the AON network include:

■ its ability to cope with change – since only information rather than the network has to be revised
■ its ability to provide the project manager with information – which is needed to make decisions about the trade-offs between the project variables of time, cost, outcome and quality
■ the speed, relative to AOA networks, with which its computer versions run.

Its disadvantages include:

■ complex calculations
■ network diagrams that are not easy to follow
■ considerable training and experience for its effective use.

The significant majority of AON network applications are computer driven and associated with large and complex projects – uses which reflect both the complexity and the power of the AON system. However, this complexity also limits its use either on small projects or in its hand generated form.

A variation on the AON network is the precedence network, in which the boxes contain slightly different information, as shown overleaf.

These nodal boxes can also be connected in different ways to reflect the complex constraints of the network and examples of these are also given overleaf.

While there can be little doubt that the computer driven AON and precedence networks represent a significant increase in terms of power and ability to cope with large and complex projects, there can

Earliest start time	Activity duration	Earliest finish time
Activity description		
Latest start time	Float	Latest finish time

Precedence network node

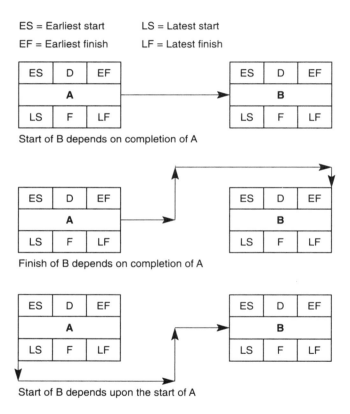

ES = Earliest start   LS = Latest start

EF = Earliest finish   LF = Latest finish

Start of B depends on completion of A

Finish of B depends on completion of A

Start of B depends upon the start of A

Examples of precedence network nodal connections

also be little doubt about the substantial premium, in terms of training, that needs to be paid to enable these networks to be used and understood. Nevertheless, AON and precedence networks are popular – perhaps because of the current availability of personal computers in our workplaces – and can make significant contributions to the ways in which our projects are managed.

Resources

So far we have only looked at the process of planning the project's use of time and the tools that we require to do that. What we now need to look at is how that project will utilise its physical resources and how we can plan our use of these. None of the types of project plan that we have looked at so far take account of the physical resources needed for the activities involved. They all assume that the resources needed to complete the activities are available:

■ in the required numbers or quantities
■ at the right time.

But in reality these resources are often in use elsewhere on the same or other projects or available in numbers or quantities insufficient to ensure activity completion in the time planned. Part of the reason for these dilemmas lies in that fact that, as we saw in Chapter 2, the resource demands of the project can vary significantly throughout its life cycle with the demands of the adulthood stage often exceeding those of the earlier and later stages by several orders of magnitude. But this is not the only cause and these shortages can also come about because we fail to plan properly either the quantities or availability of the project's resources. So when, for example, we plan to have an average of ten hours of computer time available per week, we might find that is not enough to complete all of the project network revisions and updates needed during the project's adulthood stage, and may even cause demand clashes during the evaluation part of the conception stage. But these complications may not always be concerned with a shortage of resources as there may also be limitations on the use we can make of resources. Examples of this might include an adhesive curing time that cannot be speeded up, no matter how many heaters or ovens are available, or the impossibility of getting ten men to dig, in one day, a hole which it would take one man ten days to complete.

In general, however, our resourcing problems come about because we are:

■ short of time
■ short of resources.

These problems can be overcome by using the following.

Activity slack

We saw that in the AOA network we looked at earlier we were able to adjust the way in which we undertook an activity by:

- delaying the start of the activity and using original resource level
- or by using the original start time and extending the activity duration by using fewer or different resources.

These are typical examples of what is often called 'resource levelling'. This enables the pattern of project resource usage to be smoothed with fewer and smaller peaks and troughs. The process is simple enough to be undertaken manually for small projects with limited ranges of resources. However, as the project size or resource range grows, the process of resource levelling becomes increasingly complicated. As a result, computerised systems are commonly used for large or complex projects.

Previous experience

Often when we are faced with project resource allocation problems there just isn't time to undertake a reasoned and logical analysis. This is particularly true of the resource problems which abound in large, complex and changeable development projects in which it would take too long to look at all the options and choose the best solution. Under these circumstances we can use our experience in the form of 'rules of thumb' (heuristics). These are rules which:

- are based on previous experience
- have proved to produce results which are good but not 'the best'
- are easy to understand and apply.

These methods of solving project resource problems are usually in the form of rules about which of the resource demanding activities should be undertaken first. Examples include:

- do critical path activities first
- do activities with most subsequent critical path activities first
- do activities with most subsequent activities first
- do activities with highest resource demands first
- do activities with smallest float first
- do shortest activities first.

These and other 'rules of thumb' represent simple and realistic solutions to resource problems, which can be quickly and cheaply applied.

Computers and project planning

There can be little doubt that the advent of cheap and small personal computers which are also fast and powerful has radically changed the ways in which we plan our projects. In the past decade or so the type of computer used to plan our projects has changed from a slow and physically large piece of equipment surrounded by experts and technicians to one which sits on a desk and is a commonplace feature of all our offices. Projects that were, for cost reasons, planned laboriously and manually are now computer planned without a second thought, using powerful and sophisticated software.

ᵃ Pause for reflection ᵃ
'The computer is the locomotive of the Information Age.'
Tom Peters

All of this should have led to:

- better quality project planning
- better project performance.

75

But we still have projects, as the Channel Tunnel and the British Library projects have shown us, which exceed their budgeted costs and are completed years beyond their planned completion dates. So do we conclude that the use of computers is not helping us to achieve the better projects that we have been led to expect? At least part of the answer to this lies, as we have already seen, in the fact that unsuccessful projects often have diffuse or unclear objectives or are managed with scant regard for the nature or complexity of their outcomes. The other part of the answer is that the computer is a tool and, as is so with all tools, the results it generates are dependent upon the skill of the user.

However, computers in one form or another are here to stay and they can and do make substantial contributions to the ways in which we plan and manage the successful project. In order that they may do so we need to ensure that we have:

- the right hardware
- the right software.

In both of these areas the marketplace offers a plethora of goods which are forever changing and mutating as technology and market forces drive us towards the next and better versions. This book will not attempt to influence your purchases in that marketplace or guide you towards a 'best buy'. However, what it will do is to provide a check list which will help you to begin to clarify your needs. This first step towards finding a system which will satisfy your needs is an important one – and one that is often overlooked or given scant attention in the helter-skelter rush to buy the 'new' model. Try to remember that faster or more features doesn't necessarily mean better, and always ask for the names of satisfied users and a trial copy so you can get an unbiased view and hands-on experience before you buy.

COMPUTER PLANNING CHECK LIST

1 Project factors
Think carefully about the size and complexity of the projects you intend planning for and try to identify their characteristics. For example:

- do they involve more than 100 activities or multiple resources?
- is there a high level of uncertainty about activity durations?
- will you need to update the plan frequently?
- will you need to keep outsiders well informed?
- if so, at what level of detail?
- will resource smoothing or allocation be needed?

2 Software factors
Think about your experience of project planning to date and try to identify the characteristics of the planning software that you want. For example:

- which type of plan do you want it to be capable of:
  - AOA networks?
  - AON networks?
  - Gantt charts?
  - all of them?
  - any two of them?
- what is the maximum number of activities and nodes that you want it to handle?
- do you want it to be user friendly, with menus, help screens, etc.?
- what range of calendar time do you need?
- what limitations will you accept on the way that you can identify activities and/or nodes?

- do you want it to be able to:
  - smooth or allocate resources ?
  - handle costs ?
  - plan sub-projects ?
- what sort of outputs/reports do you want?
- do you want a readable but comprehensive manual?
- are you going to need software support?

3 Hardware factors
You may have little choice about what computer and printer you use to run the software. If this is the case, make sure that you know about your existing computer and its speed, hard disk capacity, RAM size and operating system, and check that they are compatible with the software that you are thinking of using before you finalise your choice. If you can choose your hardware, think about:

- what hardware and systems you are already familiar with
- what you need as distinct from what you want
- what sort of printer capability you need in terms of dots per inch, pages per minute, operating cost, etc.
- whether you need a plotter as well as a printer.

77

Summary

- *A project plan enables us to convert project objectives into concrete realities.*

- *A successful project plan needs the skills and abilities of people to make it come to life.*

- *The first step in creating a plan is to list:*
  - *the actions needed*
  - *completion and start times*
  - *people and resources needed.*

- *Plans can be:*
  - *Gantt charts*
  - *activity on arrow (AOA) networks*
  - *activity on node (AON) networks.*

- *Each of these has its own set of advantages and disadvantages.*

- *Small projects use Gantt charts or AOA networks.*

- *Large or complex projects use AOA or AON networks.*

- *Resources can be planned and managed by:*
  - *resource smoothing*
  - *heuristic rules.*

- *Computers are key to the process of planning large and complex projects.*

6

Leading your project

Overview

Successful projects need successful project managers and this chapter looks at the nature and demands of the project manager role and its considerable influence upon the success of the project.

Objectives

By the end of this chapter you should have a better understanding of:

■ **the role of the project manager**
■ **skills and abilities that the project manager needs, including the ability to:**
  – **communicate**
  – **motivate**
  – **organise**
  – **lead**
  – **make decisions.**

Projects and project managers

A project is a parcel of activities dedicated towards the attainment of a unique goal. But these activities will not happen spontaneously – they involve people and these people will need to be managed, driven, cajoled, persuaded and motivated towards that goal. Nor will the resources that these people need appear accidentally – their arrival (and departure) will need to be carefully arranged, planned and managed. Often the project itself will need to be defended, sold or championed against the inroads of the 'politics' and intrigue that abound in our organisations and their relations with external bodies or authorities.

All of these and many more activities are the responsibility of the project manager or project leader. One of the more popular public images of the role of the project manager is that of a driven, demanding, bull-headed individual who pushes both others and himself or herself inexorably in order to gain results. Other, perhaps more cynical, views of the role of project manager (and the reasons for his or her appointment) might include:

- wide organisational experience
- knowledge and experience of organisational 'politics'
- demonstrated aptitude for keeping senior management happy
- being a good 'team player'
- availability at the 'right' time
- ability to work 'miracles'.

But, in fact, the role of the project manager is not a sinecure, a final resting place of 'burnt out' managers or even a haven for modern-day versions of Genghis Khan. This project manager role is both demanding and exciting and exerts significant influence upon the success of the project. A good project manager can transform a moribund project into a dynamic and growing entity, while a bad project manager can transform a lively and hopeful expression of someone's hopes and desires into a boring, mundane, almost routine set of activities. The most significant *raison d'être* of the project manager role is the efficient and effective management of the ways in which the project objectives are reached, and the individual selected to carry out this role must have either demonstrated this ability or have the potential to do so. But, as we saw in Chapter 2, in carrying out that role the project manager has to balance the demands and needs of:

- the client
- the project
- the project team.

In doing so the project manager must, at all times, ensure that the integrity of the project is upheld. This can involve very real skill in handling the conflicts, arguments and rivalries which can both damage and limit the progress of the project and erode the definition of the project outcome, cost, duration and quality contained in the project specification. He or she will also need to be able to solve quickly the problems which occur along the project's journey to completion and be able to lead and motivate his or her team of project staff. The complexity of these demanding tasks together with the ability to manage fluctuating levels of resources mean that the project manager's job demands a rare mix of skills and abilities.

Project managers, teams and specialists

Project managers often lead teams of specialised personnel. For example, a project team for a new office building will contain:

- civil engineers
- structural engineers
- heating and ventilation specialists, etc.

Similarly, a project for the production of pamphlets on coronary heart disease will need a team which contains:

- medical knowledge
- writing skills
- printing knowledge
- costing/cost control skills.

In both of these and all other project teams the project manager must be able to:

- gain the specialists' trust
- understand what they say or write
- communicate with them
- turn this group of specialists into a team.

Inexperienced project managers often feel that they also need to parallel the experts' or specialists' depth of technical knowledge, but this is not so. It is, however, necessary for the project manager to have an understanding of the specialism that enables him or her to:

- ask the 'right' questions
- understand the answers given.

A quiet life or a merry one?

By now it should be evident that the role of the project manager is not one for amateurs or those seeking a quiet life. It is a demanding and worthwhile role which requires skill, training and experience if it is to be carried out effectively. When we compare the role of the project manager to that of the day to day or functional manager what we see is that the project manager needs to:

- integrate rather than break down into parts
- provide the means rather than oversee

81

- be a gifted generalist who looks at holistic patterns, rather than a detailed 'tunnel vision' specialist.

These differences are significant and the effective project manager will demonstrate his or her skill by the ways in which he or she behaves. Examples of effective project manager behaviour include those related to:

- **business, economic and financial issues** – such as seeking commercial advantage, exploiting opportunities to recover expenditure, looking for successful outcomes with the client, taking calculated risks, etc.
- **project planning and progress issues** – such as identifying all tasks, planning for effective use of resources, setting targets and deadlines, anticipating and responding quickly to problems, pressuring suppliers, etc.
- **people-centred issues** – such as communicating effectively, good relationships with team and client, understanding and accepting others' views and attitudes, gaining commitment from others, etc.

If the project manager is to manage a successful project then he or she will:

- be accountable for the progress and control of the project
- have clear objectives and targets for himself or herself and others.

In order to achieve those objectives the project manager must be able to:

- lead the project team with skill and ability
- communicate clearly, effectively and precisely with everyone involved in the project
- organise the required resources, people and information so that they are available as and when needed
- motivate the actions and thoughts of the project team
- take decisions quickly and effectively.

Before we look at each of these in more detail, check out how you rate yourself as a project manager by using the questionnaire opposite.

Project managers and leadership

All project managers are leaders. They lead teams of people who may:

- be attached to the project either on a part-time or full-time basis
- only be team members for as long as their skills and knowledge are needed by the project

HOW GOOD A PROJECT MANAGER ARE YOU?

Under each of the headings below ring a number which is nearest to the way that you manage your projects and then add up your total.

1 Leadership

| I always lead my team the same way. | 1 2 3 4 5 6 7 | I try to work out which way will work best for this team and this project. |

2 Communication

| I tell people what I think. | 1 2 3 4 5 6 7 | I listen when people talk and they listen when I talk. |

3 Organising

| These things usually sort themselves out. | 1 2 3 4 5 6 7 | People have to know what to do, when, and how to do it. |

4 Motivation

| We pay them – isn't that enough? | 1 2 3 4 5 6 7 | I see my team as creative problem solvers. |

5 Decision taking

| I let problems solve themselves. | 1 2 3 4 5 6 7 | I decide quickly and with the information that I've got. |

Key:

Total

5–15	You seem to be having problems.
15–25	Well done – use your low scores to identify where you need to do better.
25 – 35	You either walk on water - or aren't being honest.

- only be members of that team for the duration of the project
- have been 'borrowed' from other departments or functions
- have substantial career investments elsewhere in the client organisation.

The project manager will also need to be involved in the selection of that team – in order to ensure that the relevant functional skills are present – and in the transfer, at the end of the project, of the team members into other roles. Much has been written and said about the process of leading others, and views about the 'who', 'what' and 'how' of the effective leader have changed over the passage of time. The traditional view was that leaders were born rather than made or trained and that these unique 'born to lead' individuals had particular features of mind or character which fitted them for the role of the leader. The assumption was that if you had these characteristics then you were able to lead – in any situation or with any group. It was also said that if you didn't have these characteristics then you would never be a leader. However, extended research over the decades has failed to support this elitist view of leadership and has been unable to identify any meaningful qualities or characteristics which are present in all leaders. As the process of leading others has at its core the ability to influence their thoughts and actions, it follows that there may be some ways of doing this that are more effective than others. Our own experiences tell us that we respond better to those who are attentive, friendly and open rather than those who are inattentive, hostile and closed.

❧ *Pause for reflection* ❧

'A leader is a dealer in hope.'
Napoleon I

Writers on leadership have identified a large number of ways of influencing others and an equally large, if not larger, numbers of ways to describe them. Many of these descriptions, such as the autocratic or the democratic styles, are broad and generalised in nature, while others, such as integrative or pragmatic styles, are more easily related to everyday ways of behaving. Some of the dimensions of these ways of influencing others are illustrated opposite.

84

Absolute authority	Consultation	Shared authority
Telling	Selling	Delegating
Leader controls	Shared control	Group control

Dimensions of leadership

It is, perhaps, not surprising to find that, despite the many studies, researchers have failed to identify the holy grail of leadership style – that one unique style which will always produce the best results. However, these studies do tell us that other factors such as:

- the setting in which the leadership was being applied
- the nature of the task
- the ways in which those being led like to be led

are just as influential as the style of the leader. Our own experiences confirm this when we reflect upon how different our responses to a leader might be under, for example, battlefield conditions or under workaday office conditions.

85

This evolving view of leadership takes our journey to the point where we can begin to see that effective leadership results when the leadership style matches the needs of:

- the given task
- the work group.

This means that there is no unique 'right' style of leadership – only styles which work better with certain groups undertaking certain tasks. This view agrees with contemporary views of the leader as a role which encompasses the more general roles of a facilitator or an enabler rather than those of a driver or a boss. It also agrees with the increasing awareness of the contributions made by the people who make up the organisation rather than those who are seen as or act as its leader.

If we accept this view of leadership – and there is substantial evidence to support it – then the 'right' way of leading a project is a question of judgement. However, if that judgement is to reach the goal of a successful project, it must take into account a number of factors, including:

- the nature of the project
- the project team composition and experience
- prior experience of project manager and project team
- constraints such as time and money.

At its core, effective project leadership is about producing results and doing so as and when required.

Project managers and communication

High among the skills needed by a project manager is the ability to communicate. Project managers spend a lot of their time communicating with others. That process can involve explaining to, informing, selling to and persuading others. It is undertaken with a very wide range of people, which will include senior client management, contractors, project team members, union officials, government inspectors and many others.

The process of communication is often thought of as a one-way process – as in telling someone something or listening to someone. But in fact all communication is *always* a two-way process. For example, even when the project manager is giving the project team instructions – about what to do next or how to do it – that team, even though the members are not speaking, is giving the project manager feedback. This non-verbal feedback, which is often called 'body language', might be shown in the expressions on team members' faces, how they are sitting or standing and whether they are looking at the team manager. Such feedback will show:

- whether the message had been heard
- whether the message was understood
- what the team member felt about the message (or the project manager).

The twin elements of the message and the feedback are essential to the process of communication – without the presence and acceptance of feedback we cannot be said to be communicating in any real sense of the word. The project manager communicates with others, as we all do, whenever he or she writes to, speaks to and even looks at others. That communication is almost always undertaken because we want to affect the ways in which others act or think. The project manager will, for example, wish to:

- instruct the project team clerk to prepare a progress report
- give information to the client manager on project progress
- seek information from a potential contractor on costs
- influence all members of the team to perform well.

All of these will involve the act of communication, and we can communicate by using the medium of the written word, as in our letters, memos and reports, or by the spoken word, as when we speak to each other over the telephone. As we have already seen we can also communicate by means of our gestures, movements, expressions, postures and gaze.

❧ *Pause for reflection* ❧

'Communication, to be effective, cannot be a haphazard process.'
John Adair

If the project manager's communications with others are to be effective, then they will:

- use a means which is appropriate to both the circumstances and the content of the messages
- take into account that others may:
  - not use the same jargon or even language
  - be physically distant from the project manager
  - not be available to receive the message.

For example, a message from the project manager to a technical specialist on the project team and containing important cost or technical data may:

- be written – so that data are communicated without error and a record of the message is kept
- use relevant technical language or 'jargon' – so that the technical issues are communicated
- be written in such a style as to reflect the relationship between the project manager and the specialist, as in 'Dear Jack', etc.

However, a message from the project manager informing the project team clerk that he or she is going to visit the subcontractors may be:

- verbal – so that the message is sent and received quickly and as a reflection of its content
- informal in style – as to reflect the relationship between the project manager and the clerk
- sent when the project manager and the clerk are able to speak to each other.

87

These and other communications will *not* be effective when they:

- are carried out in a noisy or badly lit environment – in which people cannot hear or see well
- use inappropriate language or media – that people either misunderstand or cannot understand
- do not acknowledge the presence of feedback.

Skill in the 'art' of communication is a must for all project managers. They all, if they are to be effective, must be able to write, speak, listen to and read body, spoken and written language with skill. Effective communication can make a considerable contribution to the success of the project.

Project managers and organising

88

The ability to organise is another skill which the project manager needs in order to contribute to the success of the project. In Chapter 4 we looked at the ways in which the project team and its relationship with the client can be structured, and we concluded that the choice of the 'right' arrangement for these involved:

- judgement
- knowledge of what has worked in the past
- a good understanding of the nature of the project outcomes, risks, costs, duration and special technology or knowledge needs.

We also saw that the first and essential steps in organising the project involve the generation of the project:

- specification
- roles and responsibility definitions
- budget and accounting procedures
- change control procedures.

Project managers who organise well have projects which have:

- clearly defined and understood goals, sub-goals or targets
- a detailed and comprehensive plan
- a set of priorities which are:
  - understood by all involved
  - clear
  - observed throughout the project.

These projects will also have systems and procedures which enable the project team and contractors to regulate and control their activities in ways which are:

■ effective
■ consistent
■ efficient.

These procedures are often contained in a project manual and may be concerned with:

■ type of contract to be used (lump sum, reimbursable cost or schedule of rates)
■ contractor evaluation, selection and control
■ planning and scheduling methods to be used
■ costing and accounting procedures.

These procedures should not, however, be written in rigid terms or with excessive control in mind. Instead they should provide a firm foundation on which team members can use their discretion and initiative, and the project manager has a key role to play in their creation – often at a very early stage in the project's life cycle.

Evidence of a project manager's ability to organise can often be found when we look at the project's meetings. In a successful project these are focused on:

■ monitoring progress (see Chapter 12)
■ agreeing future actions
■ identifying accountability

rather than acting as forums for excuses, politics and evasion. Good project meetings are:

■ chaired by the project manager
■ purposeful
■ kept to a previously issued agenda
■ recorded in brief minutes which state:
  – actions agreed
  – who is accountable for those actions
  – action completion targets
■ limited to a maximum duration of 1.5 hours
■ attended by a maximum of ten people
■ seen as useful, informative meetings.

Bad project meetings are:

- unfocused or without clear objectives
- attended by too many people
- too long
- run without an agenda or minutes
- seen as a waste of time
- chaired by someone with inadequate skill or authority.

A project manager's organising skills are often seen in the small details of a project, as, for example, in the presence of agendas for progress meetings or the issue of a calendar of future meetings in the early stages of the project. Nevertheless, it is often the quality of these small matters which can either speed the project on to success or bring it grinding to a halt.

Project managers and motivation

The question of what motivates people to work and to do so effectively is not an easy one to answer. Early approaches focused in on the view that the more that you reward someone then the harder that person will work and were concerned with the effects of such issues as wage levels, piecework rates, pension plans and fringe benefits such as health insurance, company cars and subsidised education. However, none of these factors, either when applied unconditionally or conditionally via a link between pay and performance, provide the complete answer to our question. While there can be no doubt that the money that we earn for our labours is important, there is also a substantial body of evidence that tells us that people work for other than their economic needs. One of the more easily understood versions of this approach was generated by Abraham Maslow. He started from an assumption that we all seek to be fulfilled and happy people and that work is one way of achieving this state. He went on to say that we all have five basic types or 'sets' of need and these needs can be arranged or 'stacked' in such a way (see the diagram opposite) as to reflect the order of their action upon us. He also tells us that the influence that these needs exert upon us is most potent when those needs are unsatisfied.

From the diagram opposite we can see that our need for warmth, food, water and shelter has to be satisfied before we begin to seek 'higher' needs such as job security, prestige and the freedom to create. However, the degree of influence or 'potency' of the needs can be and often is influenced by our prior experiences. So, someone who had long periods of being without the basics of adequate food, warmth and

**Physical and psychological
well-being**

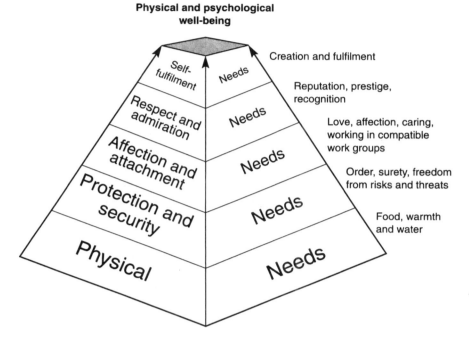

Creation and fulfilment

Reputation, prestige,
recognition

Love, affection, caring,
working in compatible
work groups

Order, surety, freedom
from risks and threats

Food, warmth
and water

The hierarchy of needs

water in the past will rate the fulfilment of this basic need above all
others and may well have diminished or limited expectations for
other 'higher' needs. Similarly, a person who has a high need to be
creative may rate fulfilment of this need above others and consequently have diminished expectations for reputation, affection and
even shelter and food. So how does this picture help us with our question about what motivates people to work and to do so effectively?
While it is almost an oversimplification to unconditionally apply this
simple need structure to the enormous complexity shown by people
every day, it does, nevertheless, provide us with some key information. It tells us that people need to be allowed to answer their social
and creative needs as well as being able to have food, warmth, shelter
and security.

❧ Pause for reflection ❧
'All that we do is done with an eye to something else.'
Aristotle

The project manager who ignores these other 'higher' needs does so at his or her peril and it is a wise project manager who recognises and allows for people's needs to:

- plan and control their own work
- be involved in the management decisions about that work.

Project managers need to be able to motivate all the people involved in the project but particularly the members of the project team. Teams are associations of people and we will look, in more detail, at the nature of those teams, how they work and their contribution to the project later in this book (Chapter 7). At this point, however, we need to be aware that project managers can motivate these team members to perform better by either enlarging or enriching their roles.

Role enlargement is concerned with increasing the scope of the role by extending the range of its duties or responsibilities. An example might be the enlargement of a project electrical engineer's role by the addition of responsibility for the project computers. Role enrichment also involves the allocation of additional duties to a role, but duties which are more interesting or challenging. An example might be the allocation of responsibility for decisions about contract allocation or client liaison to an assistant project manager or specialist project role.

However it is achieved, enhanced motivation is a vitally important issue for all project managers. It is a simple but powerful truth that well motivated project staff perform well and in so doing contribute to the success of the project.

Project managers and decision taking

We take decisions in order to settle or resolve issues or problems which are in dispute, doubt or uncertainty. All managers are involved in taking decisions and these can be about resources, such as 'how much do we spend on this?' or about policies, such as 'when do we launch our new product?' They can also be about people, problems, change or negotiations, and they can be about minor issues such as whether to have tea or coffee or major issues such as whether or not to build a new factory. The involvement of the project manager in this potpourri of decisions is no less than that of the functional manager. Decisions need to be taken about project staffing levels, about priorities, about ordering equipment, about planning and about what will or will not be done next week – and all of these have to be taken within the time frame of the project and with due regard to their effect upon the key project dimensions of time, money, performance and quality.

Decisions are taken by individuals or by groups of people, and the size and composition of the group will influence:

- the quality of the decision
- its acceptability to those who implement it.

The decisions associated with a project can be taken by:

- the project manager on his or her own
- the project manager after consulting others
- the project manager and client together
- the project team meeting with the project manager in the chair.

Whoever is involved, a vital ingredient in the decision taking process is that of information. In an ideal world, we would, when taking our decisions, have all the information that we needed when we needed it and would then be involved in a decision making process which had the following stages:

- **identify the uncertainty or problem** – such as 'What do we have to eat tonight?'
- **identify objectives or targets** – such as 'quick snack' or 'three-course meal'
- **collect and analyse information** – such as 'what have we got in the fridge?' or 'what's in the freezer?'
- **identify alternatives** – such as 'beans on toast' or 'prawn curry'
- **choose alternative to be implemented** – 'beans on toast'
- **implement** – slice bread, turn on toaster, find tin opener, etc.

In reality, the project manager often has to take these decisions when he or she doesn't have enough information or when that information is doubtful either in terms of its accuracy or its quality. The constraints of time and cost may also mean that improving that information will either take too long or cost too much in relation to the potential benefits of the decision. Under these circumstances the project manager may well be forced into settling for a 'good enough' decision rather than the 'best' decision. One way of doing this is to use the following process:

- **identify the uncertainty or problem** – such as 'What do we have to eat tonight?'

- **identify the minimum objectives or targets** – such as 'hot food'
- **collect the limited information available** – such as 'we have one can of beans, half a loaf, a frozen prawn curry and some cold, left-over roast beef'
- **identify those alternatives which can be supported by this information** – such as 'beans on toast' or 'prawn curry'
- **analyse these one by one until one meets the above minimum objectives** – 'beans on toast'.

This process does not produce decisions which can be said to be the 'best' or even the 'most favourable', but it does produce decisions quickly and from limited or even suspect data. Several other techniques for solving the dilemma created by inadequate information data are described in Chapter 10 and these can be applied by both groups and individuals. We also saw in Chapter 3 how the ranking method can be used to make the choice of which project to implement, and this method can also be applied to other decisions which the project manager faces.

Whatever method is used, the project manager must be able to take decisions – often under pressure – and the ability to do so can make a considerable contribution to the success of the project.

Summary

- *The project manager is a key factor in the success of a project.*

- *The primary task of this role is the efficient and effective management of the ways in which the objectives of the project are attained.*

- *The role of the project manager is a demanding and stimulating one which demands a rare mix of skills and abilities.*

- *The project manager must be able to:*
  - *integrate rather than divide*
  - *provide the means rather than oversee*
  - *see the 'big picture' rather than the detailed tunnel vision view.*

- *Project managers must be able to:*
  - *lead and motivate teams*
  - *communicate*
  - *organise the required resources, people and information*
  - *take decisions.*

7
Project teams

Overview

An effective and efficient project team is a key factor in the success of any project. This chapter looks at the nature and variety of the team and how it makes its contribution to the success of the project.

Objectives

By the end of this chapter you should have a better understanding of:
■ the nature of teams
■ what they do
■ the differences between teams and groups
■ the influences of team size, maturity, behaviour and membership
■ the contribution of teams to the project.

Teams

In the previous chapter we saw that the successful project manager is:

■ an integrator
■ a manager who is able to:
  – enable others
  – lead and motivate
  – communicate
■ an organiser
■ a decision taker.

Finding a person who has all of these skills and abilities is not an easy task. When you have found him or her you then have to get that person interested in your project and willing to work for you. Even when all that has happened, he or she can still fall ill, step under the proverbial bus or even leave you to work for someone else.

These difficulties and risks illustrate why teams are popular in our organisations. An effective team is not dependent on the skills and abilities or even the presence of one member – it can tap into the skills and abilities of all its members and use them to synergise a greater whole. Teams are able to grow and change to meet new demands and can reinvent themselves when individuals move on. All of us, at some point in our lives, have experienced working in a successful team – either on the sports field or in the workplace – and this experience tells us that a 'good' team can 'move mountains'. Our experience also tells us that the occurrence of these 'good' teams can often owe much to serendipity and that they can perform well and then mysteriously fall apart and break up in dissension.

In this chapter we will look at what a team is, how it works and, finally and most importantly, the potential contribution of the team to the process of managing successful projects.

What is a team?

The word 'team' is one which, despite its everyday use, can mean different things depending upon who uses it and where it is used. One obvious and common example of its use is to describe the assemblies of people who combine their individual efforts to play soccer, rugby, basketball and many other sports. In a different environment our organisations use this word to describe the crews of people who work in the same department or section and who are usually involved in some sort of joint action. 'Team' can be used to describe small groups of people, as, for example, in a marriage partnership, or large groups of people, as in a sports or work situation. When we look at these and other teams we find that, by and large, most of them:

- are structured with defined functional roles for members – as in 'goalkeeper' or 'team leader'
- work in ways which are constructive and productive – as in 'team spirit', 'team work' and 'team player'.

One example of this is the quality circles of our organisations, which have facilitator and team leader roles and are often seen as major contributors towards the process of continuous improvement. But these positive outcomes of team effort do not always occur and the behaviour and actions of teams can produce other results. They can, for example, be used to inhibit, suppress or overwhelm the initiative and creativity of individuals, both inside and outside the team. Teams can also create and foster internal social mini-environments with their own group mind-sets and their own unique collection of delusions and illusions. Teams that behave in this way are often said to be suffering from 'group think' – a malaise which causes them to waste time and money and which can lead them to think and act in ways remote from the 'real' world. A well known example of this type of team malfunction was the abortive Bay of Pigs invasion of Cuba in 1961. The Kennedy administration team for this project developed a plan:

- with assumptions that were never seriously challenged
- which was supported by an assumed consensus
- which was carried along by the president's charisma.

The result was, of course, an unmitigated disaster.

However, despite its faults, the team is here to stay as a feature of all organisations. The reason for this is simple and is that, at its best, the team is one of the most flexible and productive mechanisms for the empowering and enabling of the people who work in and make up those organisations. The results of this empowerment are not only desired by and valuable to our organisations, they are also essential to the success and the efficient operation of our projects.

97

What does a team do?

We saw earlier that the word 'team' is used to describe a wide variety of gatherings or collectives of people who are involved in a broad assortment of activities and for an extensive range of reasons. However, the activities of the teams of our organisations can be grouped under three headings:

- **Information teams.** These gather and collate information and then generate recommendations. Examples include study teams, quality circles and teams of management consultants.
- **Production teams.** These create products and services. Examples are manufacturing cells, scaffolding teams and social work teams.
- **Managing teams.** These organise and manage people and resources. Examples include executive committees, supervisory boards and project teams.

And yet, despite this diversity of purpose and activity, all of these teams do have a number of basic features in common. These are that their members:

- share an objective or desired outcome
- co-operate with each other in order to achieve that objective or outcome.

But isn't this the same as that other common collective, the group? The answer is no – the group and the team are not the same and when we look at the ways in which they are defined and work we will recognise the differences between them. For example, a typical dictionary tells us that a group of people is an 'assemblage or collection of persons' who might be:

- in close physical proximity – as in a group of commuters or a group of runners
- similar to each other in some way – as in a group of computer bulletin board users or a group of business school professors.

This typical dictionary also begins to indicate one of the differences between the team and the group when it tells us that the team is a collection of people who 'collaborate in their professional work or in some other enterprise or assignment'. These differences become even more obvious when we probe into the numerous studies that have been conducted on groups and teams. These tell us that when we compare the group to the team what we find is that:

Group members:
– have purposes in common
– undertake individual actions
– generate individual outcomes
– exert influence

Team members:
– have shared purposes
– undertake co-operative actions
– generate collective outcomes
– create defined, measurable team 'products'

These studies also tell us that while groups frequently have leaders – a role which remains with a single individual who can be formally appointed or evolves informally – leadership in teams is generally less formal, often shared and the leader role can move around the team depending on availability of individuals or the task in hand. Teams are also seen to have 'untidy', open ended problem solving debates while groups have efficient and orderly meetings which delegate work to others often outside the group.

> ❧ *Pause for reflection* ❧
> **Look at the section, department or office that you work in or lead and decide whether it is a team or a group**

By now we are beginning to see that one of the significant qualities of a team is its ability to tap into and harness the efforts, skills, abilities and creativity of all its members towards the achievement of a shared goal. As such, teams have a considerable potential to contribute to the success of our projects. However, if we are to grasp this potential and turn it into a reality then we have to make sure that we have a team which has:

- the right size
- the right members.

Little or big teams?

We have already seen that our sports teams can vary from the 15 of a rugby union football team to the pair of a tennis doubles team and this range of team size is extended further when we look at the teams of our organisations. Sales teams can, for example, consist of as many as 30 individual salesmen and the teams associated with large projects can often reach 20 or so members. While the size of these teams is often related to the staffing needs of the task involved, there are, nevertheless, important issues about whether these large teams can:

- allow all their members to communicate effectively with each other
- take decisions and solve problems in such a way as to use the skills and knowledge of all team members.

Small teams, for example, allow their members to communicate easily with each other and the skills, creativity and knowledge of all members are usually harnessed towards the solution of problems. In larger teams, however, effective communication is often limited to a vocal (and dominant) minority with the less confident members or those with minority views being less able (or willing) to contribute. Nevertheless, whatever the quality of the communications in the large team, these teams do have a bigger pool of knowledge, skills and experience to draw on than the pool of the smaller team, which is, inevitably, more limited. When we try to decide what the 'right' size is for our project team, we have to bear in mind:

- the demands of the project task
- the higher levels of skill, knowledge and experience that would be present in a larger team
- the higher levels of member involvement and commitment that would occur in a smaller team.

> **⋙ *Pause for reflection* ⋘**
>
> **Is your team too big?**
> **Do people feel able to contribute at**
> **meetings without 'barging in'?**
> **Do a minority hog all the 'air space'?**

Many teams have been studied over the years and this research tells us that there are considerable benefits to be gained from limiting the team size to a maximum of ten people. It is also apparent that, on projects in which member participation and involvement are key issues, such as joint union/management study groups, the team size should be limited to between five and seven members. If we reflect on the above we begin to see that if we want to harness the efforts, skills, abilities and creativity of our team members towards the shared goal of a successful project then we have to limit the size of the project team to between six and eight people. This may mean that, on large projects or projects with high manning levels, we need to organise our project so that we have a series of interconnected teams with the smaller satellite teams connecting to the main team like the plantlets of the spider plant. Main team members will chair or lead these satellite teams and take responsibility for the smooth and easy flow of information between the main and satellite teams. Getting the size of the team right is not, however, the only factor that contributes towards an effective and efficient project team. We also have to make sure that what is sometimes called the 'chemistry' of the team is right.

Team chemistry

Teams can sometimes be comfortable work spaces and at other times they can be difficult, uncomfortable and unpleasant spaces to work in. The factors that influence the ambience or atmosphere of these teams do so in ways which are complex and not always fully understood. In order to create and run our project teams so that they make an effective contribution to the success of the project we need to be aware of a number of these factors.

Team maturity

Teams are dynamic organisms made up of people; as a result they change and develop throughout their lives. In the early stages of the team's life the members will often be strangers and their responses to each other's actions and the demands of the team's task will be:

- individual rather than co-ordinated
- based on their prior experience.

As time passes the differences between individuals will become more evident and, as a result, power struggles, fights and conflicts will occur. Gradually, however, the team will begin to integrate and members will start to develop a commitment to the team and its task. As this increasingly cohesive team builds up its stock of shared experience, members will have the opportunity to establish their team roles and work together with increasing effectiveness. Finally, when the task is complete, the team will break up and disband.

ह **Pause for reflection** ह

Which stage is your team at?

During each of these stages the team will have a different:

- ambience or atmosphere
- level of productivity.

For example, during the stage in which power struggles, fights and conflicts are prevalent, the atmosphere in the team will be tense, uneasy and unproductive. However, if the team passes through this unpleasant but inevitable stage and moves into the next stage, its atmosphere will become constructive and productive, with co-operation becoming normal behaviour.

Team behaviour

The ways in which people behave in teams are, in essence, no different from the ways in which they behave outside them. As we saw in Chapter 6, the ways in which people behave are motivated by a number of needs, and the actions of these needs upon us are complex and often unconscious. When we work in teams our behaviour is shaped or influenced by:

- the team task
- and/or the behaviour of other team members.

For example, while in a team we will take decisions, give and seek information and opinions, agree and disagree with others, and test and summarise our understanding of what others have said – all in pursuit of task completion. We will also encourage others, score points off them, attack them, seek recognition from them, defend ourselves from what we see as their attacks and even temporarily withdraw from the group – all in response to the influence of the behaviour of other team members.

≈ Pause for reflection ≈

Are attack and defence the norm in your team?
or
**Do team members feel free to test ideas,
thoughts and feelings?**

102

The expectations that team members have of each other's behaviour are often called the standards or 'norms' of a team. Each team will have a different set of these norms which are often unwritten and sometimes even unspoken. These expectations develop and change as the team develops and the social pressure on all team members to conform to them can be very strong. Failure to conform with them will result in pressure from the rest of the team and ultimately expulsion. The power of this pressure to conform must not be underrated – it can easily and quickly reduce even strong and tough minded individuals to fuming impotence but it can also ensure that team members who are less strong and outgoing are given the space and freedom to express their views.

Team members

For many of the teams of our organisations the members are selected on the basis of their functional skills, i.e. on the basis of the job that they do while not in the team. On other occasions and in other teams people might be chosen for team membership because they:

■ are easy to get on with
■ do what they are told
■ don't rock the boat
■ think the same way as the selector.

However, none of these ways of selecting people for team membership will result in a team which is effective or efficient in any real sense of those words. What they will succeed in producing is a team:

- which does not have a balanced set of skills
- the members of which do not feel that their particular skills and abilities are used to full effect.

If we are to have a successful team then all of the team members will need to have skills other than those related to their area of functional expertise or attributes other than their similarity to the team selector. All team members will, for example, need to be able to:

- make decisions
- solve problems
- co-operate with other team members
- display and use relationship skills with other team members.

Selection solely on the basis of the potential team member's functional role or other attributes gives us little assurance about the presence of these other vital team skills. What we need to do when we choose our team members is to choose them not only for their ability to:

103

- use their functional skills
- make decisions and solve problems

but also, and more importantly, for their ability to integrate their particular and individual package of skills into that of the team. This task of integration into the team is not an easy one for any of us – we have to give up a part of our individuality in order to gain access to the greater whole of the team – but it is one which can be achieved. Indeed, our own experience tells us that this process of integration can be made easier when we pick up and use the roles which an efficient team needs. These roles are concerned with:

- generating ideas
- defusing conflict or tension
- looking after the arrangements and chores
- challenging the team consensus
- clarifying objectives and setting agendas
- being the team analyst.

A successful team consists of a mixture of people which provides a range of individual characteristics that is adequate to ensure that enough different team roles are carried out. The presence of these roles will result in a team which is:

- not dependent upon any one member
- resilient and adaptable
- able to produce results.

When you are choosing your team members you can get information about them from a surprising range of sources, such as:

- the ways that they have performed in other teams
- their responses to training and development programmes
- what their current or former bosses think about them
- team role assessment questionnaires such as those developed by Dr Meredith Belbin or Drs Charles Margerison and Dick McCann.

The task of selecting a team is key to the success of that team. Without the right mixture of skills, abilities and experience the team will not be able to contribute to the success of the project and may even break up in dissension and conflict. However, with the right mixture, the outcomes of the team will exceed that which would be expected from the sum of the abilities and skills of its individual members.

104

꒰ *Pause for reflection* ꒱

Do you pick your team members
– because you like them
or
– because they'll do a good job?

Project teams

The role of the team in the management of a project is a key, if not vital, one. The level of the effectiveness and efficiency with which the actions, decisions and outcomes of the project team are carried out makes a considerable difference to the ways in which the project inputs of:

- information
- people
- resources

are managed and used. They also make a considerable difference to the way in which the project manager is able to balance the often conflicting needs and demands of:

- the client
- the project
- the project team itself.

Earlier in this chapter we found that teams are different to groups and can serve as a focus for powerful forces acting towards the achievement of shared goals. All of this applies equally to project teams.

However, at first glance the composition of the project team will appear to be defined by the needs of and nature of the project task. For example, a training and development project whose outcome is a new training programme for middle managers on project management will need a team which contains people with skills and knowledge in:

- **the subject**, i.e. project management
- **client subject needs**, i.e. the project management needs of middle managers
- **how to design the programme so that it meets those client needs**, i.e. programme structure design, programme material design and programme material visual aid design
- **how to market the programme**, i.e. potential client lists, mail shots and advertising
- **how to administer the programme**, i.e. client registration, fee payment, hand-out material, printing and copying
- **how to deliver such a programme**, i.e. lecturing and seminar skills, credibility with clients, etc.

However, this and all other project teams need and demand other skills than those associated with members' external functions or roles. Project teams also need to have members with:

- decision taking and problem solving skills
- interpersonal skills

and who are willing to integrate these skills into the greater whole of the project team. However, most of the books about project management pay limited attention to the importance of the ways in which the project team functions, preferring to discuss and identify the formal structures and organisation of the team and its relationships with clients, contractors and others. Consequently, and not surprisingly, most project teams are almost exclusively focused on the project's functional needs. We often have project teams of people who are good structural or piping engineers or teams of people who are, for example, excellent social workers, nurses or administrators but rarely do we have project teams of people who are good at their functional role *and* good at being a team member.

The importance of achieving a balanced and integrated project team that can harness the skill and abilities of its members to create a whole which is larger than the sum of these cannot be stressed too strongly. A project team with this capability can overcome what appear to be overwhelming difficulties, trials and tribulations and ensure the success of the project. Use the questionnaire below to check out your project team.

HOW GOOD IS YOUR PROJECT TEAM?

Under each of the headings below ring a number which is nearest to the way that your project team operates and then add up your total.

1 Goals and targets
No goals or targets are evident   1 2 3 4 5 6 7   Goals and targets are clear and well defined.

2 Decisions
No decisions are made.   1 2 3 4 5 6 7   Decisions are made on the basis of full consensus.

3 Team resources
Contributions are limited and no dissent is expressed.   1 2 3 4 5 6 7   Everyone is fully engaged and effectively used.

4 Leadership
There is no clear leadership.   1 2 3 4 5 6 7   The best person for the task leads.

5 Team process

No attention is
given to the way
we do things.

1 2 3 4 5 6 7

We always try
to find better
ways of working
together.

Key:
Total

5–15   This seems to be more like a group than a team.

15–25   Good – check your scores with the rest of the team
and use the results to focus your joint efforts in
order to improve.

25–35   See if the rest of the team agree with your scores – if
they do you are either a top class team or all suffering
from terminal group think.

107

Summary

- A good project team is essential to a successful project.

- The members of these teams:
  - have shared purposes
  - undertake co-operative action
  - generate collective outcomes
  - create defined, measurable team 'products'.

- Effective teams usually have between six and eight members with a maximum size of ten.

- Teams are not static – they develop, change and grow.

- The stages of this process have different ambiences and levels of productivity.

- Team members should be chosen for:
  - their functional skills
  - their decision making and problem solving skills
  - their skills in working with other team members.

Project estimates and budgets

> *Overview*
>
> **Money has been described as the 'lifeblood' of all projects. This chapter looks at the ways in which the money needs of projects are estimated and budgeted for and the contributions that those processes make to the successful project.**
>
> *Objectives*
>
> **By the end of this chapter you should have a better understanding of:**
> - **the need to estimate accurately the cost of your project**
> - **some of the ways in which those project costs can be estimated**
> - **how the accuracy of those estimates varies during the project life cycle**
> - **how project budgets are created and what they are used for.**

Money, money, money

Our use of money has its origins in the early history of humankind and is evident in all civilised societies. And yet the coins and notes that we use for money have, in themselves, little intrinsic worth and their value, for us, lies in their use as a medium of exchange. We exchange money for the food, houses, cars, clothes, holidays and books that we want and we exchange our time, skills and abilities for the money that we call our salaries or wages. Money invades almost every aspect of our lives and acts as the supreme enabler. Its presence enables us, for example, to have choices about:

- what we do
- when we do it
- what we use to do it with.

Our proverbs and sayings illustrate the power of money when they tell us that:

- **'money is power'**

- **'money is the sinews of war'**

- **'time is money'**

- **'money is the root of all evil'.**

In our projects the pervasiveness and power of money are no less than in the rest of our lives, and money is a unique and special resource which affects every aspect of the project's operations. Its presence enables us to purchase or hire the equipment, tools and materials that we need and to ensure that the right people with the required skills and abilities are available when we need them. Its absence means that we might run out of materials when we need them or that we might not have enough of the right sort of people or equipment to do the tasks that we planned to do. It enables us to:

- plan our projects
- create our project teams
- buy or hire the equipment that we need
- buy the materials that we need
- create the outcomes of the project.

109

In short, we would not have a project without the enabling power of money. However, its presence is not an unconditional guarantee of a project's success and we have to ensure:

- that we have enough of it to satisfy our project's needs
- that it is available when we want it.

This chapter looks at how we can answer those needs by the ways in which we:

- estimate
- budget for our project's money needs.

Guesses, estimates, assumptions and presumptions

When we estimate an object's worth we are, in fact, assigning or attributing a value to that object, and we usually do so by comparing that object to similar or identical objects for which we know the value. Similarly, when we estimate how long we will take to complete a task we do so by comparing that task to other similar or even identical tasks that we have previously completed. But estimation is not just a process of comparison, we also need to use our judgement about the information that we have about that task and the circumstances under which it was undertaken. For example, when we see that a task is twice the size of the last one we did, do we automatically double the hours that we needed last time or do we allow for the fact that we have, by repetition, learnt to do the task quicker? Similarly, when we need to estimate the cost of printing a book, do we increase the cost from the last one we produced in proportion to the number of pages these books have or do we allow for the fact that:

■ the cost per sheet of paper falls when we buy more
■ and most of the printing machine time is taken up in setting the machine up rather than printing the pages?

The skill with which we exercise our judgement about these and other matters can make a considerable difference to the accuracy of our estimates and ultimately to the availability of the money which the project needs to succeed. Successful projects are based upon estimates which take into account:

■ the project's objectives and outcomes
■ the activities which are needed to achieve them
■ the historic costs of similar or identical activities.

But, as we saw in Chapter 2, the information that we have about the project's activities varies considerably throughout its life cycle. In the initial conception stage of the project we find the level of information available is very low and this will only rise when we have passed through the birth and development stage into adulthood. As a result, the accuracy of the estimates that we can generate during these stages will differ. For example, in the conception stage we will have little detailed information and may, at the beginning, only have an approximate size or other dimension for the project outcomes. These outcomes can, as we saw earlier, vary enormously in their nature and characteristics, and examples of the limited information that we have at this stage might only tell us that our project is about:

■ improving the morale of about 300 employees
■ or creating a pamphlet about coronary heart disease
■ or building a new factory like this one
■ or creating a new training programme for managers.

The limitations of this information often mean that we can only produce an estimate which is indicative rather than definitive and, as such, has a considerable potential for error. Estimates of this type are given a variety of names such as:

■ ball park estimates
■ seat of the pants estimates
■ order of magnitude estimates
■ guesstimates.

All of these graphically illustrate the potential for error of these estimates, which can be as much as 30 per cent or more. Nevertheless, this type of estimate, which involves little time or cost in its generation, is often used:

■ to gauge management interest levels in the project
■ in early planning decisions.

However, their use in anything other than very preliminary decision taking is fraught with risk.

111

More and better information

What often happens as a result of the generation of a ball park estimate is that a decision is taken to:

■ drop the project
■ or develop it further.

The decision to develop the project will lead to further design and other activities which will cause more information to become available. As a consequence we are able to convert our earlier examples of project outcomes into the following:

■ a programme for raising the morale of the 307 employees of the Hove factory of the XYZ company and to be held in August 1997
■ the creation of a four page A5 pamphlet about how to reduce coronary heart disease risk by diet and exercise
■ the replication of a Croydon factory on a green-field site in Brighton
■ creating a new residential three day training programme on project management for middle managers.

This increase in information enables us to create estimates of greater accuracy; these are generally called:

- preliminary estimates
- predesign estimates
- or feasibility estimates.

These estimates are also often used to decide whether to proceed with the project, and their potential for error will depend upon the amount of information available. In high cost or high risk projects much preliminary design work will be undertaken, leading to an estimate of ±15 to 20 per cent accuracy. However, the estimates for smaller, less complex or lower risk projects will be based on:

- limited preliminary design work
- comparisons with similar projects.

This may have an accuracy band as wide as ± 25 per cent. However, once we have decided to proceed with our project, we will then become involved in further decisions about and work on the size, scope and nature of its outcomes and these will generate the more detailed information which, as we saw in Chapter 4, forms our project specification. This higher level of information enables us to generate the last of our estimates, which is generally described as the:

- definitive estimate
- or project control estimate.

This has a potential for error of ± 5 to 10 per cent. It is used to generate our project budgets and, as we will see in Chapter 12, provides the baseline for our efforts to monitor and control the progress of our project.

ᐖ Pause for reflection ᐖ

What is the accuracy of your project estimates?

Estimate data sources

It will be already evident that the accuracy of our estimates is very dependent upon the accuracy of the information that we have about our project and its outcomes. This consists of:

- information about those outcomes
- information about the costs of generating those outcomes.

The first of these, the outcome information, grows in terms of its content and level of detail as the project passes from the conception stage of its life cycle to its birth and development stage. The project specification, as we saw in Chapter 4, is the definitive version of this information and provides a clear and unambiguous statement of the project's baseline. It is from this baseline that we develop our project's:

- final definitive estimates
- budget
- plans and schedules.

The presence of this outcome information, whatever its form and level of detail, is crucial to the generation of the second information source – about the costs of outcome generation. Starting from the outcome information, the process of creating the generation cost information draws upon a rich variety of sources, which can include:

- records of previous projects
- suppliers' catalogues
- quotations from suppliers and contractors
- your organisation's standard costs
- trade and government cost indices
- trade magazines
- professional journals and publications
- reference and text books
- industry standards
- the experience of you and your colleagues.

113

The skill and judgement that is exercised in the use of these various information sources is crucial to the accuracy of the project's cost estimate. But, however well those sources are used, the accuracy of this estimate is, in the end, primarily dependent upon the accuracy of the information about the project's outcomes. If that is wrong or inaccurate then our estimates will be at least as wrong and inaccurate.

Estimate scope and contents

All estimates, whatever the quality of their information sources, have a number of basic constituents.

Labour costs

These can be expressed as:

- direct costs
- or indirect costs.

Direct labour costs are those which can be directly ascribed to a particular project activity or part of the outcome, whereas indirect costs or overheads relate to the overall business of running the project as a whole. The administration and management costs of the project are often described as overhead labour costs and include the costs of the project manager, secretaries, clerks, etc.

Material cost

Most material costs are, in one form or another, direct costs. The materials involved will, of course, depend upon the nature of the project outcomes, but examples of the materials involved might include:

- building projects – bricks, concrete, sand, wood, glass, tiles, etc.
- training projects – paper, overhead projector transparency film, textbooks, pre-recorded and blank video tape, etc.
- equipment installation projects – electric cable and ducting, piping, building materials, etc.

Equipment costs

Equipment may be needed because it is:

- part of the project's outcomes – as when our project has the outcome of a new computer system
- or to achieve those outcomes – as when we need scaffolding to retile the roof of our office block.

This equipment can be:

- hired
- leased
- purchased outright.

Each of these will have different cost implications. Whatever the purpose of your equipment and however you acquire it the project estimate will need to contain the relevant costs.

Insurance, taxes and other charges

The estimate will need to include the costs of insuring project staff and equipment against injury, loss or damage and providing protection against claims for loss and damage from other people as well as any tax liability. Other charges made against the project might include such fees as:

- design charges
- consultancy fees
- inspection fees.

Most of these are usually considered to be overhead costs.

Inflation allowance

As we saw in Chapter 3, the value of our money changes with time and we need, if the life span of our project exceeds six months, to make allowance for this in our estimates of project cost. This can be done by using government and industry predictions for the rate of cost inflation. However, with projects of an extended duration this process can leave the project manager at risk and it may be necessary to build in a cost review clause which allows for the sanctioning of additional funds in the event of inflation indices exceeding a defined level.

115

Contingency allowances

All estimates are, by their nature, attempts to predict future costs, and sometimes these predictions can be wrong. This can occur, for example, when:

- mistakes or errors are made
- information and costs are omitted
- new information becomes available
- costs increase at rates above the inflation rates allowed in the project budget
- exchange rates fluctuate
- earthquakes, typhoons or strikes occur.

The project estimate can include an allowance to cover for these and other events and this is called the contingency allowance. The size of this allowance is typically 5 per cent but can be influenced by a number of factors, including:

- amount of previous experience with the type of project
- project risk level
- technology risk level
- likelihood of events such as earthquakes, typhoons or strikes.

The contingency allowance is not intended to cover for:

■ changes in scope
■ bad estimating.

It is intended, however, to provide cover for unknown or difficult-to-predict events.

&. *Pause for reflection* &.

Look at the estimates of your last project and check whether you allowed for all those basic constituents.

or

Use the check list below to review your estimating.

116

PROJECT ESTIMATE CHECK LIST

Does your project estimate include:

1 Overheads such as:
■ design fees?　　　　　　　　Yes ☐ No ☐ Not relevant ☐
■ consultancy fees?　　　　　Yes ☐ No ☐ Not relevant ☐
■ insurance costs?　　　　　　Yes ☐ No ☐ Not relevant ☐

2 Labour costs such as:
■ project manager/team costs?　Yes ☐ No ☐ Not relevant ☐
■ direct labour costs?　　　　Yes ☐ No ☐ Not relevant ☐
■ sub-contract labour?　　　　Yes ☐ No ☐ Not relevant ☐
■ temporary labour?　　　　　Yes ☐ No ☐ Not relevant ☐

3 Material costs such as those needed for :
■ electricity, heating or ventilation
　supply?　　　　　　　　　Yes ☐ No ☐ Not relevant ☐
■ any building work?　　　　Yes ☐ No ☐ Not relevant ☐
■ special materials such as:
　– computer network wiring?　Yes ☐ No ☐ Not relevant ☐
　– pre-recorded videos?　　　Yes ☐ No ☐ Not relevant ☐

---

4 Equipment costs such as:

■ purchase cost?	Yes ☐ No ☐ Not relevant ☐
■ hire cost ?	Yes ☐ No ☐ Not relevant ☐
■ lease costs?	Yes ☐ No ☐ Not relevant ☐

5 Contingency allowance?   Yes ☐ No ☐ Not relevant ☐

6 Inflation allowance?   Yes ☐ No ☐ Not relevant ☐

Notes

It is impossible for a short check list to cover all the details of all the possible projects that the reader might have, *but*:

■ if you have less than two yes's, then you might have a problem
■ if you have 16 'Not relevants', then you definitely do have a problem.

How do we estimate?

The enormous variety of project outcomes means that a considerable number of estimating techniques or methods have evolved, each of which has value and relevance for a particular type of project outcome. The following represent some of these techniques.

Exponential method

This method is often used in the early stages of the project, when limited information is available about the detail of the project outcomes. However, the following must be available in order to use this method of estimating project costs:

■ some factor which tells us the size or capacity of the project outcomes – such as the number of pages in a book, the floor area of a house or the duration of a training programme
■ historic cost data for a project with a similar outcome.

This information is used to estimate the cost of the new project by applying it in the following formula:

cost of new project = cost of old project $\times$ ($S_{new}/S_{old})^{0.66}$
where S_{new} = size or capacity of new project
S_{old} = size or capacity of historic project.

This tells us, for example, that when the cost of producing 200 copies of a 150 page book was £3,500, the cost of producing the same number of copies of a new but similar 200 page book will approximate to:

$$£3,500 \times (200/150)^{0.66}$$
$$\text{or} \quad £4,232.$$

If we had ratioed these costs in direct proportion to the size of the books we would have estimated the cost to approximate to:

$$£3,500 \times (200/150)$$
$$\text{or} \quad £ 4,666$$

which is over 10 per cent more.

Care must be taken in using this method to ensure that proper comparisons are being made. It would, in our book example, be wrong to use the cost of a paperback book with line drawing illustrations to estimate the cost of a hardback book with coloured photographs.

Learning curves

We have already seen that one of the key characteristics of a project is the uniqueness of its outcomes. This uniqueness may be such that it involves us in activities that we have not undertaken before, and when we estimate the labour costs of these new tasks we need to take into account what is often described as the 'learning curve'. This tells us that our performance gets better when we repeat a task, which means that our work output will be low when we are unfamiliar with the task but will rise as we become more familiar with it. This applies whether we undertake the task once in each of our projects or whether we repeat it several times in a single project. In its basic form the learning curve tells us that the mean time for a repeated operation will decrease by a fixed fraction as the number of repetitions doubles. For most tasks this fraction lies between 80 per cent and 90 per cent, which means that if we take 70 hours to do the task the first time, then the second time will take 70×0.8 hours and the fourth time $70 \times 0.8 \times 0.8$ hours and so on until the mean time approaches a steady value.

❧ Pause for reflection ❧

Calculate the task times for the above example at 8, 16, 32, 64 and 128 repetitions.

If you plot these figures on graph paper you will find that the curve begins to flatten out after about 100 repetitions at a value of about 17 hours. If we had based our estimate on this figure, which represents the time an experienced person would take, then for 50 repetitions we would have budgeted for 50 × 17 = 850 person hours. But our learning curve data tell us that at 50 repetitions the average time would be about 19 person hours, giving us a total of 950 person hours. This means that if we had ignored the effects of the learning curve we would have underestimated the time and cost by almost 12 per cent. The mathematics of applying the learning curve to our estimates of project cost are made easier by using ready-made tables, which are illustrated in most operations management textbooks.

Beginnings and ends

We have already seen that the levels of project activity differ as the project moves through the different stages of its life cycle. When we look at the activities which make up the project we find that these also display levels of activity which start low, rise and then fall as the task begins, reaches a steady state and then approaches its completion. These differing activity rates will obviously influence the labour that we need for the task. For example, when we have a task which requires a total of 400 person hours and needs to be completed in two 40 hour working weeks our common sense might tell us that we can calculate the number of people that we need by dividing the people hours by the hours available, i.e. 400/40 × 2. This tells us that we need five people. But we have ignored the effects of the differing activity rates that occur, and we can allow for these by assuming that:

- the build-up or start-up phase lasts for 20 per cent or two days of the ten available
- the run-down phase lasts for 30 per cent or three days of the ten available
- the peak activity level occurs during the remaining five days
- during both the start-up and the run-down phases activity changes between zero and the peak activity level in a linear manner.

When we add together these different activity rates we find that:

400 people hours = (2 days/2 + 3 days/2 + 5 days) × 8 hours/day
× peak number of people
or the peak number of people = 400/7.5 × 8 = 6.66 people.

So, if we had assumed a constant activity rate our estimate would have been too low.

Factorial estimating

This impressive-sounding title disguises a simple method of estimating cost which is often used on engineering projects. In its most basic form it starts from a detailed and accurate cost for the main project outcome and multiplies this cost by factors to generate the cost of the ancillary outcomes. For example, if we find that the cost of a new boiler is £10,000 then by the use of factors we can estimate the cost of:

- the piping as £10,000 × 0.36 = £3,500
- the instruments as £10,000 × 0.18 = £1,800
- the foundations, etc. as £10,000 × 0.26 = £2,600

and so on. Simple as it may appear, factorial estimating needs, if it is going be accurate, factors which are based upon large amounts of historic cost data. It also needs to be applied with a degree of judgement which takes into account the idiosyncrasies of both the historic and the new projects.

Budgets and budgeting

The individual cost estimates and allowances that we have generated are brought together in an overall statement of project cost called the project budget. But this is more than just the accumulated sum of our estimates. This budget is used to:

- identify the likely cost of project implementation
- tell the client organisation how much money needs to be sanctioned
- tell the project manager how much money is needed and when it is needed
- provide a datum level against which project expenditure can be monitored and controlled.

In order to achieve these the project budget must tell us not just what is to be spent but also when it is to be spent. In doing so the budget draws heavily on the content of the project plan, which, as we saw in Chapter 5, tells us what are the:

- start points

■ finish points
■ durations
■ people and equipment demands

of the project activities. Indeed, this connection between the budget and the project plan, is so close that it can be argued that the budget is an extension of the project plan and as such itself forms a plan for money allocation throughout the project's life span.

As such the budget plays an important role in the management of any project. It enables the project manager to see what money is needed to implement the project plan and when it is needed. It also, with the project plan, plays a key role in the process of monitoring and controlling the project, and this is what we look at in Chapter 12.

Summary

■ *The creation of accurate estimates and budgets is a vital factor in the success of the project.*

■ *Types of estimate are:*
  – *ball park estimate (± 30 per cent)*
  – *feasibility estimate (± 15–25 per cent)*
  – *definitive estimate (± 5–10 per cent).*

■ *Estimates must include:*
  – *labour costs*
  – *material costs*
  – *equipment costs*
  – *insurance, tax and other charges*
  – *inflation allowance*
  – *contingency allowance.*

■ *Estimating techniques include:*
  – *exponential method*
  – *learning curves*
  – *activity profiles*
  – *factorial estimating.*

■ *Budgets are plans for money usage.*

■ *Budgets enable projects to be:*
  – *monitored*
  – *controlled.*

Projects and change

Overview

All projects have the target of creating change, and the ways in which that change process is managed can make a considerable difference to the success of the project. In this chapter we look briefly at the nature of change itself and then explore the ways in which it can be managed, with particular reference to their use in the project.

Objectives

By the end of this chapter you should have a better understanding of:
- the nature of change
- the ways in which it can be managed
- the importance of its effective management to the successful project.

Change – here and now

The project is just one example of the process of change in which we are all continually immersed. Indeed, the commonalty of this process is such that we often accept it or take it for granted on an everyday basis. We are, for example, exposed to (though often not without comment) the changes in the weather which occur not only with the passing of the seasons but also with the hours of the day. Similarly, as we age, we experience (though not always happily) the changes that gradually occur in our bodies and which limit our abilities to lift or run as well as we did when young. But not all of the changes that we experience are as automatic as the weather or the process of ageing. We can also induce or create change in our lives from choice or as a result of a decisions that we take. We can choose to wear different clothes, change our jobs, have different hair styles, live in a different house and even change our partners – and do so by the exercise of our will. This process of change by choice is often an expression of our individualism and is a significant factor in the ways by which we manage our lives. But, whether started by choice or not, all of these changes have consequences, and these can be:

- significant or small
- trivial or traumatic.

In our management of the project it is our ability to manage the consequences and implications of these changes which is so vital to the success of that project. In order to find out how that process can be successfully managed we first need to look at the nature of change itself.

Change – what is it?

The typical dictionary tells us that change is the substitution of one thing for another or the succession of one thing in place of another. However, this substitution or succession can:

123

- result from the exercise of our own free wills, impulses or choices
- be forced or imposed upon us as a result of the choices and decisions of others.

Generally our experience of change includes both of these types of change. For example, while we can choose whether or not we take our next holiday in a part of the world which is new and unknown to us, we cannot choose whether or not we pay increases in income tax or value added tax. We can also choose whether or not we stop eating meat and become a vegetarian, but we have to accept the changes in our travelling plans which result from a strike of railway signalling staff. But the issue of whether we are or are not a party to the choice or nature of the change involved can make a significant difference to our response to that change. For example, a change that we have chosen is one that we will feel positive about and respond constructively to, even when it goes wrong or does not occur quite as we planned. On the other hand, a change that is forced upon us generally leads us to react in unconstructive ways, which can involve resistance, conflict and even sabotage. This negative reaction to involuntary change is one that occurs irrespective of the nature or value of the change and needs to be taken into account when we look at how we manage the change process of our projects.

Change – temporary or permanent?

When we think about the changes that we experience in our lives we will find that these differ in a number of ways. They can, for example, be:

- **short-lived, temporary or even cyclical** – as in the seasons of the year
- **relatively long-lived and stable** – as when we get married or change our job
- **reversible** – as when we change the morning newspaper that we buy
- **irreversible** – as with the invention of the bicycle, the transistor, the motor car or the computer.

Many of the changes that we experience are short-lived and transitory in nature – as when we have a shower of rain or a temporary hiatus in our cash flow situation – and after these have passed we revert back to the original status quo. Other changes, however, are more stable and long-lasting and demand deeper and more radical changes in the ways in which we order our lives. The influence of the real or perceived duration of a change is significant and can make a considerable difference to the ways in which we respond to that change. If, for example, we realise that a change is short-lived and unlikely to persist then our reactions are those of temporary adaptation or accommodation. We will, in effect, do as little as we need to do in order to adapt to the presence of that change. Our responses to the presence and passage of that change will be passive – we will bob up and down as we would on an ocean wave. If, however, the change is irreversible and long-lived then our reactions will be more proactive. For if we are to be successful in our management of that change and its consequences then we need to reach out and embrace the change and integrate it into our lives – and the project is a powerful mechanism for doing just that.

124

ê Pause for reflection ê

Think about a change that you have recently experienced and try to identify if it was:
– voluntary or involuntary
– reversible or irreversible.

Projects and change

We have already seen, in Chapter 2, that the project is primarily concerned with creating change. The ways in which that change occurs and is managed can make a tangible and major contribution to the achievements of the project. Yet most of the traditional project management textbooks ignore this vital aspect of the project management. But, when we look at the role of the project manager in real, rather than academic, terms, there can be little doubt that to be successful the project manager must be an effective change agent. This means, in its simplest terms, that she or he must be able to operate in a frame of mind for which change is normal, rather than a cause of panic or alarm. Only then, when change is embraced rather than held at arm's length, will the full potential of the project come to fruition, and only then can the project manager act as both helmsperson and manager and so ensure that the powerful process of change is focused on the success of the project.

The outcomes of that process are, for our projects, changes that are rarely trivial or insignificant and they often warrant a considerable investment of organisational time, money and energy. Nor are these outcomes ephemeral – they are created for the long run, often in support of that organisational goal of continuing survival, and as such can represent irreversible quantum leaps forward for the evolving organisation. But, as we saw at the beginning of this book, these projects can also have outcomes which are more modest in nature and finite in duration – but outcomes which nevertheless are, for the work group, team or department, also:

- significant
- focused on the long run
- concerned with the creation of 'steps forward' from which return would be difficult and expensive.

But how do we get this to happen successfully and what must we do to ensure that the change process is managed effectively?

Equilibrium and change

One of the early and major contributions towards our views of the ways in which we can manage the process of change came from a social scientist called Kurt Lewin. He expressed the view that individuals and organisations behave as they do because of the effects of arrays of opposing forces. Our behaviour and that of our organisations represent an equilibrium between the forces that seek to pull or push us in opposite directions. But neither our behaviour nor this equilibrium are static or frozen – they are both dynamic and active expressions of our interactions with the world around us. That world is continually changing, and as a result the forces that create the equilibrium also change. Only a small change in any one of these forces is needed to generate a disequilibrium or imbalance, with a consequent movement or change which continues until equilibrium becomes re-established in a new position. The forces which act upon that equilibrium situation will, of course, be situation specific – i.e. they will depend upon the situation involved. They and the situation are generally portrayed as shown below.

126

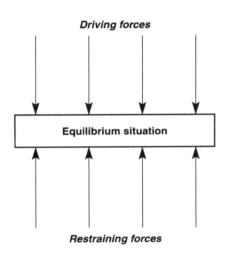

Force field

While these forces rarely act in one to one opposition to each other, they can, because of the complexity and ambivalence of human affairs, represent mirror images of each other. One example of this is where we feel both fear and excitement when faced with a change. One of these, fear, acts to restrain or inhibit us from change while the other, excitement, seeks to push or drive us towards the change, and these are the mirror image of each other. The forces which create the equilibrium can be anything that is relevant to the situation. When we use this way of looking at change on our projects we find that these forces can be concerned with any of the inputs to the project process, which, as we saw earlier in Chapter 2, are:

- information
- people
- resources.

They can also be concerned with any of the key dimensions of the project, which are:

- time
- quality
- cost
- performance.

When we want to create change we have to change this equilibrium and start a process which has three stages:

- destabilise the current equilibrium
- shift to a new position
- restabilise the new equilibrium.

The initial step of destabilisation requires us to:

127

- identify the forces
- decide what change we want
- choose the force to be adjusted
- weaken or strengthen that force as required.

You can use this technique, which is called force field analysis, on your own or with groups of people. It enables you to:

- identify what to do next
- reduce what appears to be a large problem to one which can be handled
- get the people involved in the change on the same wavelength.

In the project, we have already seen that these forces will include the often opposing needs and desires of:

- the client
- the project team
- the project manager.

We will look at the ways in which the consequent conflicts can be resolved in the next chapter. In the meantime, however, we will take a brief look at the ways in which that vital project input of people reacts to change and how we can ease the path to change by managing the process of its introduction.

People and change

Projects are truly people-centred – they are sequences of activities that rely, whatever the nature of their outcome, on the creativity and skills of people to ensure both their completion and their success. But, by and large, people don't like change – they resist it and cling on to the wreckage of the old, rejecting the clean, uncluttered fresh start of the new. So how do we overcome this fear and thus enable our project to be powered to success by the energy and creativity of its people?

In order to answer we first look at why people don't like change and then use that as a stepping stone for our successful management of the project change process. Research tells us that people dislike and avoid change primarily because they fear it or its consequences. This fear can be generated by a number of real or imagined factors, including:

■ the new and unfamiliar
■ the unknown
■ the absence of trust
■ involuntary and enforced involvement
■ potential for loss
■ the need for surety and certainty
■ previous bad experience of change.

Our experience will also tell us that people may also resist the change because they:

■ think that it doesn't makes sense
■ see it as containing errors or mistakes
■ feel it ignores important issues or factors.

But people can also be enthusiastic and positive about change, and the reasons for this can include:

■ the excitement of the new
■ the potential rewards to be gained by changing
■ voluntary involvement in the choice of change
■ trust in the change agent
■ previous good experience of the change process
■ familiarity with the nature of change
■ the potential penalties suffered by not changing.

They may also support the change because they:

■ agree with its aims and objectives
■ see it as contributing to a greater good.

John's dilemma

John realised that he was facing a difficult situation - the student registrations on the programme for managers of leisure centres, which he ran at the Dingleberry Business School, were falling and he needed to do something about it. A casual chat over coffee with Ron, his head of department, had indicated that the programme might be axed, unless registrations increased. John felt that this was unreasonable – after all, at least five students had graduated each year over the last decade – but he also knew that Ron, underhand ambitionist that he was, meant what he had said. So, faced with the threatened curtailment of his flagship programme, John applied his mind with some vigour. Some hours and a bottle of malt whisky later John had a flash of inspiration – 'What about using force field analysis?' he said to his mate Fred, who, being wise, said little. And so they applied themselves with more vigour and some hours later had generated the following diagram.

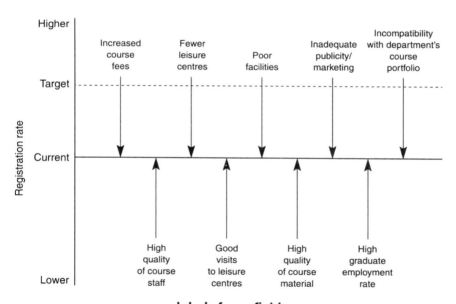

John's force field

'Now', said John, 'we're getting somewhere. What about a new glossy programme brochure, mailshots to all local authorities within 100 miles and a mid-term visit to that new indoor arena in Houston, Texas!' Fred, being wise, said nothing but sighed inwardly at the thought of yet another long night of John's creative genius.

If we are to manage our project so that it achieves change success-fully then what we have to do is to take a leaf from Kurt Lewin's ideas about change and:

- eliminate or reduce the fear and other negative factors
- increase the positive factors.

Making it happen – the key factors

People react in complex and often contradictory ways to the process of change, and the ways in which we manage our projects must take into account the often conflicting needs, wants, fears and anxieties of those who are involved in or affected by the changes involved. If we fail to do so then not only will we fail to achieve success, but we might also fail to achieve the desired outcomes of the project. We have already seen that if we involve people in the choices and decisions involved with the change then their reaction to that change is much more likely, in net terms, to be proactive and positive. We have also seen that when we impose change upon people then they often react negatively, with resistance, conflict and even sabotage. The polarity of these reactions leads to the point at which we can see that if we are to achieve success in the management of the project change then we must:

- encourage commitment by involvement and explanation
- encourage and allow people to take responsibility for their own actions in the change process
- give people enough information and training to enable them to do so effectively.

In order to manage this change in a way that is effective and results in the achievement of the goal of a successful project we need to co-ordinate and balance our use of the following key aspects of the change process:

- information
- communication
- people
- power.

All of these make a significant contribution to the process of managing change effectively. If we ignore even one or use them in an unco-ordinated or unbalanced way then we will fail and the resulting outcome of the change process will be short-lived, ineffective or unstable.

Before we look at how we co-ordinate our use of these key factors, we need to look briefly at each of them in turn to establish what they contribute to success in the process of managing change.

Information

Information consists of facts and figures which are meaningful. For a successful project this information will, for example, consist of facts and figures about project objectives, costs, targets, timetables and milestones. However, these facts, figures and statements will *not* be enough on their own. In order to contribute to the success of the project they will have to:

- be easily understood
- have relevance, meaning and significance
- be accessible.

The first two of these, understandability and relevance, will come about if the ways in which we communicate with others are designed and undertaken in such a way as to be effective. That links us to the next key factor of communication, while the third factor, accessibility, leads us to the factor of power.

Communication

Information on its own is not enough, it needs to be communicated to others. But this process of communication is not limited to informing others but is a two-way process in which, if it is to be effective, you have to listen as well as talk. It is also a process which, when carried out well, can make a considerable contribution to the ways in which the project change is managed. Despite the fact that we communicate with each other all of the time, doing it well is not always easy. For example, there may be situations in which communicating with all of those involved in the change process will take a long time and a lot of effort. There may also be circumstances where prior experience or history has biased or prejudiced people's views and they are reluctant to trust or listen to those who propose the change, or where the very survival of an organisation is at stake, or where the issues involved are of considerable commercial sensitivity. Each of these circumstances will influence the content and style of the communication which takes place. The need for effective communication in our projects is a continuous and ongoing one – communication is not a one-off exercise – but it is also a worthwhile one. However, important as this process of communication is, the goal of a successful project will not be achieved unless that process is used to gain people's involvement and commitment.

People

We have seen already that the involvement of people in the process of change is a 'must' if we are to achieve success. This involvement, if encouraged and allowed to grow, will lead to commitment rather than compliance and will encourage and allow those involved in or affected by the change to influence its content and progress. It does not, however, involve the project manager in abdicating his or her responsibility for taking decisions – nor is it consensus management. What it does mean is that project management creates a culture in which people feel free to ask about what is happening and management feel free to ask 'What do you think?' without feeling bound to accept the answer unconditionally. The detail of the method you use to encourage the growth of this involvement will differ with the different roles and levels of your project team. Specialist project team roles such as engineers or medical staff may need, for example, to feel that they retain their technical authority while still being exposed to the views of both their internal and external 'customers' and the needs of the project team as a whole. As we saw in Chapter 7, one way of harnessing and supporting these twin horses of involvement and commitment is by the use of the team. The project team is a powerful weapon in the process of managing change and creating the successful project. This can only take place with the support and co-operation of others, and those who attempt to impose change on others put not only the project, but also their future relationship with others, at risk. They will do so because they fail to gain the support and co-operation of those who are needed to carry out that change. This use or abuse of power is the final key factor that we shall look at.

Power

Power has been defined as the ability to do or effect something, and those who have it in our organisations decide:

- who gets what
- when they get it
- how or in what form they get it.

People can be seen to be powerful because they:

■ have a role which gives them formal authority over others
■ control or have access to scarce or high value resources such as money, information, technology or knowledge
■ have access to others with power or information
■ are seen as charismatic or influential
■ can punish or discipline others.

The project manager has power because of the formal role that she or he carries out and the control that role has over:

■ the how much and when of project spending
■ the who and when of project team recruitment
■ the how and when of information interchange with the client.

That project manager may also be a charismatic individual who generates considerable trust in those who work for him or her and who exerts considerable influence over the project team and the client.

We saw earlier that it is the co-ordination and balance of these four key factors which will lead to success in the way that we manage the changes our project creates, rather than their individual and separate influence. This balance is not only one of the ways in which our organisations display their different cultures, it is also a feature of the process that we call leadership, which, as we saw in Chapter 6, is a key factor in determining project success. What we will now do is to look at how these four key factors of information, communication, people and power can be blended into a co-ordinated and effective whole.

Managing the change process – the choices

The way that we choose to manage our project's change process will be influenced by a considerable range of factors. In making that choice we need to take into account and be aware of such factors as:

■ time available
■ previous relationships of those involved
■ risks and rewards involved
■ marketplace pressures
■ competitor activities
■ political pressures.

When we look at these and other factors we begin to realise the complexity and power of these influences. Examples of these might include:

- the bad (or good) prior experiences that both team members and the client have had with project managers – these will influence the quality of project communications
- a client with a falling market share and profitability who will need a new product project to be driven through in order to improve both of these as quickly as possible
- government demands that a local authority sets up a project to improve its customer service performance will be responded to slowly because:
  - the next election or minister may change that policy
  - the rewards are limited
  - the topic is unfamiliar.

Nevertheless, whatever the range and complexity of these influences we cannot, if we desire success for our project, avoid the need to be proactive in the ways we manage the process of change. Success will not come to those who only react to change, and we must anticipate the events, problems and difficulties of our projects if we are to be successful.

The Omega Suitcase Company

The Omega Suitcase Company was in trouble: customer complaints and returns were up and sales were down – something had to done. Managing Director Jon Hudson decided that the time had come for Omega to launch a project to improve the product quality. Previous attempts to do this had failed – not surprisingly since they had been based almost entirely on the management's view of what was wrong. Jon decided that the time had come to do it differently – but how? After some thought he decided he would have a talk with Walter Higgins, the union organiser who had retired last year and who was always to be found at lunchtime in the bar of the local hotel. Walter greeted Jon pleasantly enough and, after the initial pleasantries, Jon plunged in. He told Walter about the rising returns and the need to do something. He also admitted that management had got it wrong before. Walter smiled broadly at this and asked Jon what he proposed to do. Jon's brave and honest response was to say that he wasn't sure but he did know that it had to be done differently and it had to involve everyone - not just management. 'Good,' said Walter, 'but don't expect the lads to believe you at first.' He went on to remind Jon that little or no attempt had been made to ask shop-floor workers or supervisors what they thought in

134

previous quality campaigns and said that future attempts would, without doubt, be treated with suspicion and cynicism. 'But,' he said, 'it can be done, though it will take a long time.' Jon sat back when he realised this – he began to see that the process of managing this project successfully would, for a while at least, be a slow one and one which could only start once trust had been rebuilt.

Someone very wise once said that people don't really resist change, rather they resist being changed, and if we ignore this resistance, however it is expressed, we do so at our peril. The wise project manager will accept resistance and work with it to create an environment of trust and co-operation. The unwise project manager will ignore this resistance and may even try to enforce change by using coercion, threats and power. The results of these actions will not contribute to the success of our projects, with even the ostrich-like 'head in the sand' action of ignoring the resistance gradually but surely creating a project 'environment' in which that resistance will grow and change from the tacit to the outspoken and from covert indifference to overt sabotage. But how can we, as project managers, react to that conflict and resistance? The answer is that if we are to manage that change effectively then we do so in such a way as to gain the:

- co-operation
- support
- commitment
- involvement

of all those people involved in or affected by the change. We will only achieve this if we work *with*, rather than against, these people and if we accept and encourage their integrity and creativity. To do this *and* obtain results is not an easy task but one which is worthwhile and key to the success of the project. However, this process cannot begin until three key initial steps are taken:

- we must accept, indeed anticipate, opposition and resistance
- we must accept conflict, use it constructively and debate issues instead of contesting territories
- we must act, as project managers, in ways which clearly and unequivocally demonstrate the above.

Once we have taken these initial steps then we are ready to begin the process of implementing our change.

We have seen already that the use of power alone to crush resistance or to force others to accept a change will result in:

■ increased resistance to that change
■ reduced stability of that change
■ diminished effectiveness of that change.

Nevertheless, the result could be a rapid change, but one which is not likely to be sustainable or stable. By and large, people do not like being forced or coerced into doing things and, if they are, often retain feelings of resentment or anger about the incident. These emotions will limit their willingness to co-operate fully with the required changes. This use of power alone will not generate the permanent structural change that is required for many of our projects. Nor will the other extreme of ignoring this resistance aid or facilitate that change.

The actions that we do need to take in order to manage effectively the change which is implicit in our projects can be illustrated in the diagram below.

As we can see, we begin our shift away from the extreme of managing change by power alone by the action of sharing facts. This can

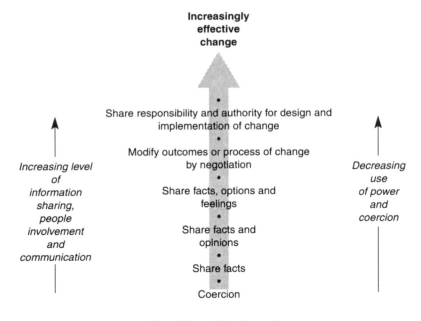

Creating effective change

evolve into the process of sharing facts and opinions and then the process of sharing facts, opinions and feelings. We can then negotiate the what, when and by whom of the change with those involved, and ultimately we can delegate and share the responsibility for making the change happen and the authority to do it with others. This increasing involvement of others is not revolution but evolution and a process by which we all are able to contribute to the vision of both the direction of the project's growth and change and the views of how that is achieved. It is, however, a process which will demand considerable skill and ability, on the part of those who manage it, in the use and harmonisation of the key factors of information, communication, people and power. The ability to resolve conflicts (see Chapter 11), plan (see Chapter 5) and solve problems (see Chapter 10) will be required, in addition to the ability to lead and communicate effectively (see Chapter 6), together with the ability to operate in teams (see Chapter 7). Failure to use all of these skills effectively and failure to achieve the correct balance of the four factors of information, communication, people and power will, at any stage of the project process, lead to a rapid descent down the greasy pole and a reversion to reliance upon coercion in one form or another. That will lead to the failure of the project.

137

Summary

- *The project is one form of the process of change that goes on around us all of the time.*

- *Effective management of that change is key to the success of the project.*

- *Change can be:*
  - *significant or small*
  - *trivial or traumatic.*

- *Change can also be:*
  - *freely chosen by us*
  - *imposed upon us by others.*

- *It can also be:*
  - *reversible or irreversible.*

- *The project exists to create change which is generally but not exclusively:*
  - *significant*
  - *irreversible.*

■ *This change needs to be managed with care and thought using tools
such as force field analysis and by a co-ordinated and balanced use
of the factors of:*
  – people
  – communication
  – information
  – power.

■ *Effective management of change:*
  – accepts and works with the resistance that people have to change
  – accepts and works with conflict
  – involves those affected by the change
  – generates their commitment.

10

Problem solving for projects

Overview

All projects have their problems. In successful projects these are
identified, analysed and solved quickly, effectively and cheaply. This
chapter looks at the nature of our project problems and reviews the
ways in which we can recognise, analyse and solve them.

Objectives

By the end of this chapter you should have a better understanding of:
- the range and diversity of project problems
- the ways in which information about those problems can be
gathered
- some of the techniques which enable us to recognise, understand
and analyse project problems
- a number of the ways in which potential solutions to these problems can be identified.

Problems

The word 'problem' is in very common usage and we often use it to
describe the situations that we encounter. We might say, for example, that we have a problem when:

- our car fails to start when we need it to get to work
- the washing machine breaks down when we need it to do the
family wash
- our computer 'loses' our work when we need to print it out
- we miss the bus or train that we needed to get to be in time for our
meeting or our class.

In all of these and many other situations we come face to face with
actual conditions that differ from those to which we aspire. It is this

gap or gulf between our wishes and the reality of the world around us that creates or crystallises what we often choose to call a 'problem'.

But is that all that it takes to create a problem? The answer to this question is that it isn't, and when we probe further into those situations we call problems what we find is that, in addition to the gap between what is and what we want, they also have other characteristics. For example, the problems we described earlier would *not* be problems if we:

- could accept the situations
- had a spare car or could get a lift
- could get the washing machine fixed quickly or
- could use someone else's machine until it was fixed
- knew how to recover the 'lost' computer file
- were able to postpone or reschedule our meeting or our class.

However, if we were unable to accept these situations or the solutions were not available then we would still feel that we had a problem. This tells us that we have a problem when we are:

- faced with a situation in which an unacceptable gap exists between what we desire and what actually is
- unable to identify or access a way of closing that gap.

The *Oxford English Dictionary* adds to this view of the problem when it tells us that a problem is 'a supposedly insoluble quandary affecting a specified group of people or a nation', or 'a difficult or puzzling question proposed for solution'. When we add these dimensions to our maturing view of the problem it becomes a gap between that which is and that which we want, which is:

- unacceptable
- difficult or troublesome
- puzzling or perplexing
- apparently insoluble.

❧ *Pause for reflection* ❧

Look at the section, department or office that you work in or lead and decide what are the key problems that it currently faces.

Problems are astonishingly common in all of our lives, both at work and at play, and when we look at our projects it is not surprising to find that they also have their problems. These can, for example, be about:

- the differences between what we planned and what we have been able to achieve
- the fact that we don't have an effective project monitoring system and consequently aren't sure about what is happening and when it is happening
- the unplanned absence, when needed, of key equipment or key people
- misunderstood messages, instructions or requests.

The changeful nature and limited duration of a project provide a fertile breeding ground for problems and for all of them there will be:

- a wide range of possible causes
- an equally wide range of potential solutions.

One of the ways in which the importance of the project manager is demonstrated is in the way that he or she identifies and solves these project problems. This means taking decisions and, as we saw in Chapter 6, the project manager must be able to take these decisions quickly and effectively in order to contribute to the success of the project. Problem decisions are about:

- what is the 'real' cause of the current problem
- what is likely to be the most effective and economic solution.

In this chapter we take a look at some of the ways in which the project manager can:

- collect
- analyse
- use

the information which is so essential to the identification and generation of an effective and economic solution to the problems of the project. However, before we take that look we first have to examine another and equally important key step – that of identifying the problem.

Problem – cause or effect?

The problems of our project can and do present themselves in a variety of ways. For example, projects often fall behind even the most carefully laid of plans and schedules, and the project manager may be presented with a set of symptoms which might include:

- work backlogs
- project milestones not being achieved
- increasing levels of stress and conflict in the project team
- high and rising levels of overtime.

The first reaction of the project manager may be to conclude that these have come about because:

- project staff aren't performing well enough
- or there aren't enough of them.

But neither of these might be the case, and alternative and equally feasible causes could include:

- poor work supervision
- inadequate task information
- poor monitoring information
- bad planning
- poor co-ordination of different tasks and roles
- lack of equipment or machines
- bad decisions by the project manager.

142

> *Pause for reflection*
>
> **Look at the workplace problems that you identified earlier and see how many possible causes you can identify for each problem.**

At this stage it is worth reminding ourselves that, as we saw at the beginning of this book, all projects have the primary inputs of:

- information
- people
- resources.

All of these can and will contribute to our project problems. However, the first step towards solving those problems lies not with jumping to the most obvious conclusion but with the key action of identifying what is the real, rather than the apparent, problem.

Which problem?

One of the ways in which we can identify the real nature of our project problems involves the simple but methodical process of asking
the following questions:

- what is happening?
- where is it happening?
- when is it happening?
- why is it happening?

When we apply this technique to our earlier problem we begin to
get answers such as:

- what is happening? *Answer*: activities b, c, and f are falling behind
  schedule
- where is it happening? *Answer*: the main delays are evident at the
  printing stage of the production process
- when is it happening? *Answer*: the backlog became evident in week 32
- why is it happening? *Answer*: not clear, but could be:
  - raw material delays
  - poor performance
  - poor supervision
  - poor task definition
  - inadequate task information
  - inadequate equipment.

While these initial answers may not provide a clear definition of
the project problem, what they do provide is a clearer view of its possible causes. To get closer to that, what we must now do is to apply
the technique again, this time focusing upon the previous answers
given to the 'why?' question, and asking, for example:

- what raw materials are being delayed? *Answer*: red ink
- where is that delay occurring? *Answer*: at the supplier's warehouse
- when is the delay happening? *Answer*: it started in week 29
- why is it happening? *Answer*: the order has low priority with the
  supplier.

As a result of this analysis we find that the problem has changed
from an apparent labour or productivity problem to a supplier problem. The project manager can now decide to look for an alternative
supplier and/or put pressure on the original supplier to deliver.

Another way of identifying the real nature of our project problems
involves the use of what is often called the cause and effect, Ishikawa

or 'fishbone' diagram. The creation of this diagram starts with us drawing, on the right hand side of a sheet of paper, a box inside of which we write the effect that we are facing. We then draw an arrow across the sheet, pointing towards the box, and then add four further arrows which connect into the sides of this main arrow. Each of these side arrows represents one of a number of groups of causes, any one of which could have caused the effect identified in the box. These groups are usually related to the:

■ people
■ equipment
■ method
■ materials.

that are involved. When we apply this technique to our earlier project problem the result is as illustrated below.

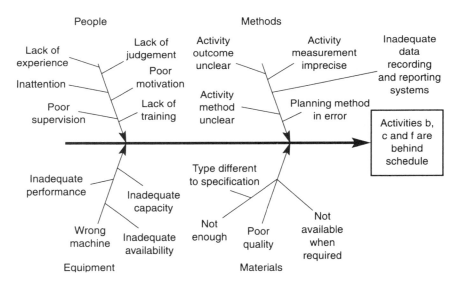

Cause and effect

The diagram above, if drawn with care, thought and attention, gives us a comprehensive list of all possible causes of the effect that we wrote in the right hand box. As with the previous question and answer technique, it does not tell us which of these is the real problem but it does stop us jumping to wrong conclusions. In order to get to the real problem this technique may need to be applied repeatedly, with each application getting into finer and finer detail.

> ❧ *Pause for reflection* ❧
>
> **Apply the Ishikawa method to one of your
> workplace problems.**

Information, data, facts and figures

Both of the above techniques will, when carefully applied, give us a more comprehensive understanding of the root causes of the apparent problem or the nature of the real problem. What we now need to look at is how we can collect and analyse the information that we require in order to:

- corroborate that the problem is the real problem and not a symptom of another, deeper problem
- identify potential solutions for that problem.

145

We saw in Chapter 6 that project managers, in common with all other managers, often have to take decisions:

- without enough information
- with information of doubtful quality or accuracy.

We saw also that, because of the constraints of time and cost, they frequently have to settle for decision outcomes which are seen to be 'good enough' rather than 'best'. Nevertheless, despite the too frequent reality of these constraints, it is also almost self-evident that the decisions we take are only as good as the information that we base them on, and that time spent in gathering and analysing information is well spent. However, in many of our projects time can be at a premium and what we need are techniques which enable us to use the available time to greatest effect. The following are among those principles and methods that have stood the test of time and extended use.

Diagramming

We can use diagrams in a number of ways to help us solve our project problems. They can, for example, be used to help us to identify all of the inputs to and outputs from a process, as shown overleaf.

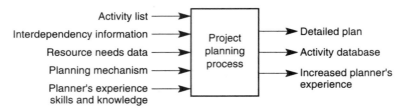

Inputs and outputs

The generation of the input-output diagram above requires that we:

■ understand the process under review
■ identify all the process inputs and outputs.

This means that our later use of more detailed or focused techniques is based on a foundation of good and comprehensive information.

We can also use diagrams to make sure that we have identified all of the causes of our problem, as shown below.

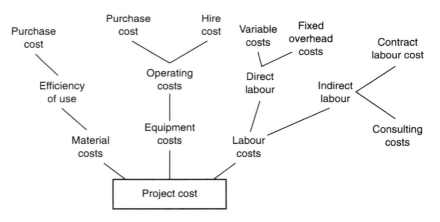

Causes of project costs

This type of diagram is often called a multiple cause diagram and can be used as a way of identifying relationships between causes and effects in project problems.

╔══╗

❧ Pause for reflection ❧

**Generate a multiple cause diagram for one of
your workplace problems.**

╚══╝

Sampling

When we need to measure what is going on, our instincts often tell us to measure everything and to generate, often at considerable cost, great swathes of data which take considerable labour to convert into meaningful information. All of this effort is not necessary. We can dip into or take small amounts of this data, from which we can draw conclusions or inferences about the rest of it. This process is called sampling and it:

- saves time and money
- speeds up our review of the available information.

This means that we can either take less time to review the available data or look over a wider field of data in the same time that it would take to look at all of one smaller part in detail. We can sample anything that can be counted or is measured, and examples of data which can be sampled include:

- activities of people involved in the project
- use of key equipment
- queues at key project 'service' points.

147

Using ratios

Using ratios will often tell us all sorts of interesting things such as:

- failure rates on key activities like welding or typing – expressed as a percentage of total output
- machine or equipment usage levels – expressed as hours in use/ hours available
- activity levels of people – expressed as hours worked/hours available

or less direct but just as valuable information such as:

- number of telephone complaints/hour
- average days of sick leave per employee
- average order value/customer.

These ratios, when generated for a number of operations, machines or tasks, draw our attention to those areas which are not being as productive as others. The potential causes of this lower productivity are legion and might, for example, include:

- defective equipment
- delays in material supply

- task difficulties
- delayed management decisions.

While these ratios will not tell us what the causes are, they will draw our attention to the need to examine an individual task, machine or operation in more detail. A powerful adjunct to the use of ratios is the 80:20 rule, which tells us that a small part of the activities (20 per cent) that we are examining will account for a large part (80 per cent) of the effects. This rule can be illustrated by looking at the staff time taken to respond to patients at a hospital accident and emergency facility. Most of the patients have minor injuries or complaints and individually absorb limited amounts of staff time. However, a small number of accidents involve major, life threatening injuries and, as such, demand and receive large amounts of staff time. Studies of staff time usage in these situations tell us that the minority (around 20 per cent) of the patients absorb the majority (around 80 per cent) of the staff time. This can be applied to any group of similar activities, such as those which take place in a typing pool or a welding shop, and goes on to tell us that the majority of the mistyped letters or defective welds will come from a minority of the typists or welders. This rule, which is also called the Pareto rule, enables us, in the above examples, to focus our attention on the unproductive typists or welders and put right whatever is causing the high failure rates. In all of our projects the 80:20 rule enables us to cut through the thickets of surplus and potentially misleading information and focus our attention and decision making on those aspects of the problem situation which will produce significant changes:

- quickly
- with minimum data.

Analysing the problem

Whatever the technique we use to identify our real problem and its associated information, we will, nevertheless, always need to scrutinise, examine and take to pieces that information and separate it into its constituent and relevant parts. This is the process of analysis, and the ways in which it is conducted can make a considerable difference to both the quality and the speed of the project manager's decision taking and problem solving process.

The following are some of the techniques which can be used to enhance both the quality and speed of the analysis process.

Average, median and mode

When we examine a group of figures it is often handy to be able to represent this group by a single figure. This can be done in several ways:

■ **Average.** This is the arithmetic sum of the group values divided by the number of items on the group as in:

Group: 9, 5, 10, 8, 25, 8, 14, 8 and 11
Arithmetic sum: 98
No. of items: 9
Average: 10.88

■ **Median.** This is value of the middle item of the group, when that group is arranged in order of size. For the above group the order will become:

5, 8, 8, 8, 9, 10, 11, 14, 25

and the median is the fifth number, 9.

■ **Mode.** The mode of a group is the most frequent item in a group, which for our example group is eight.

We can use these representative numbers in different ways. We can use the average to represent all the data in the group and we can monitor its value to watch if the composition of the group changes. The median can be used to represent the group even when we don't know the exact value of all its members but do know:

■ how many there are
■ how many are above and below the median.

Similarly we can use the mode when we only know the value of the middle items in the group or when we want to know the most likely value of a factor or variable.

Moving average

This average enables us to establish whether a factor is changing its value and in which direction. For example, in a project where the outcome is a book, the number of pages written per week might vary as follows:

Week number	No of pages written
1	12
2	13
3	10
4	15
5	17
6	9

The average number of pages written during three-week periods was:

Period	Average number of pages written
weeks 1 – 3	11.66
weeks 2 – 4	12.66
weeks 3 – 5	14.00
weeks 4 – 6	13.66

150

These moving averages enable us to monitor the trends in the number of pages written, without being misled by extreme values or by regular fluctuations in value.

✆ *Pause for reflection* ✆

Set up a moving average on one of your workplace problems. What does it tell you ?

Decision trees

When the project manager takes a decision in order to solve a problem, he or she will almost always be faced by uncertainty about the outcomes of the alternative actions available. Decision trees are often used to assess those outcomes by using the project manager's estimate of:

■ the likelihood of that outcome occurring
■ the financial consequences of that outcome.

For example, a project manager whose project is running behind schedule is faced with a decision as to whether to commit additional funds to a key activity in order to get back on schedule. The estimated likelihood of this succeeding is 60 per cent, whereas if he or she does nothing the likelihood of the project getting back on schedule is very low (10 per cent). The decision tree for this decision will be as shown below:

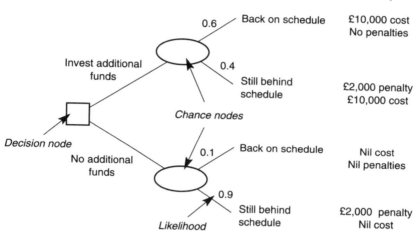

Cost consequences

A decision tree

The probable costs of these alternatives will be:

additional funds – £ (10,000 × 0.6 + 12,000 × 0.4) = £10,800
no additional funds – £ (0 × 0.1 + 2,000 × 0.9) = £1,800

These indicate that, because of the low penalty cost, the best decision is to not invest additional funds. If, however, the penalty cost rose to £30,000, then the probable costs of these alternatives would change to:

additional funds – £ (10,000 × 0.6 + 40,000 × 0.4) = £22,000
no additional funds – £ (0 × 0.1 + 30,000 × 0.9) = £27,000

This shifts the cost balance in favour of a decision to invest additional funds. Decision trees will not make your decisions for you and the results that they generate are only as good as the estimates that you make for the likelihood of the alternatives. However, they do enable you to see:

■ which of these estimates is critical
■ what are the effects of alternative values.

Answers and solutions

Whatever technique we use to identify our problems and analyse the data associated with them, we all, in the end, face the need to generate effective and economic solutions to those problems. But unique, one-off, 'special' solutions are very rare and, more often than not, we are faced with a number of alternative solutions, each of which has its own set of advantages and disadvantages. Under these very common circumstances we are faced with the task of:

- identifying
- evaluating

a solution from one of those alternatives and in ways which are:

- quick
- easy
- inexpensive.

The first step in this process is that of identifying the alternatives.

Finding the answer

The solutions to our problems rarely spring unbidden to our hands — they have to be cultivated, worked at and sometimes even forced into existence. As we saw earlier, this process can often, from necessity, take place under circumstances in which the information available is limited and/or inaccurate. The processes that we use to identify and evaluate the potential solutions to our problems must be:

- robust enough to survive this 'desert' of factual information
- able to respond to the limited data which is available
- capable of producing consistent and reliable results.

These processes include the following examples.

Brainstorming

Perhaps because of its name, brainstorming is often thought to have much in common with the process of spontaneous and sudden creativity, as in the eureka-like idea of a single person. But this is not so and the process is, in fact, a structured and consistent attack on a problem

152

which involves a group of people in amassing a number of spontaneous ideas which are then discussed and evaluated. The basic rules for this process are as follows:

- the group should:
  - not involve those who decide which solution will be adopted
  - involve as wide a range of people as possible
  - consist of between eight and fifteen people
- the group is there to identify or even create solutions but *not* to evaluate them
- *all* solutions are accepted, however bizarre, silly, illogical, impractical or ridiculous they may appear.

In its fullest form the brainstorming process has three stages.

Generation stage

This stage starts with the assembled group being briefed on the problem and one member being elected to act as the group leader. This role involves:

153

- reminding the group of the basic rules of no evaluation and the acceptance of all ideas
- acting as 'scribe' and writing down, on flip charts, all the ideas generated.

These ideas are shouted out without any explanation or justification and are immediately written down in the form of a numbered list. The duration of this stage will depend upon the experience of the group and the complexity of the problem, but about 30 minutes is typical. However, silence should not be taken as a signal to end this stage – it may well be that the group is catching its breath before another spasm of ideas. When, however, the ideas do run out the next stage must begin.

Categorisation stage

The numbered ideas are now categorised by the group. The usual categories used are:

- good
- bad
- unusual

but other alternatives are:

- possible
- not possible
- 'off the wall'.

It may help to group together similar ideas under each of these categories and to see if any of the unusual or off the wall ideas fit into any of these groups – or into a new one.

Selection stage

Group members are now asked to write down which they consider are the three most promising ideas and these are collected and collated.

> * za Pause for reflection za*
> **Set up and run a brainstorming session to identify possible solutions for one of your workplace problems.**

Lateral or sideways thinking

Most of the time when we come face to face with the need to solve a problem our thinking is influenced, even conditioned, by the extent and nature of our:

- past experiences
- knowledge.

We generally use these in structured ways to logically and systematically break the problem down into its elements and to then, by making judgements, generate a solution. But, as we have all experienced, there are also occasions when solutions appear spontaneously and illogically – as it were 'out of the blue'. Lateral or sideways thinking seeks to encourage that process and to deliberately break out of the structured patterns of thinking and to allow the process of creativity to work with the information available. It does so by:

- firstly, recognising the factors which limit or dominate your thinking – as, for example, that a project activity is always done in a certain way or that it is always followed by another certain activity
- secondly, using a number of simple techniques to incite or induce creativity – such as that of using random words or that of reversing the current view to trigger a new approach or concept.

Lateral or sideways thinking is generally used as a complement to our more conventional ways of solving problems, with lateral thinking generating the ideas which are then evaluated by conventional logical thinking.

Choosing the solution

Most of the methods that have been described will generate a number of alternative solutions to our project problems, and what we have to do is to choose which of these we are going to implement. This choice can be made in a number of ways, and the following are two examples.

Delphi method

The original Delphi method was used in technological forecasting and involved analysing the results of a questionnaire sent separately to a number of experts, who were therefore not subject to the inhibiting factors of a round-table discussion. Like brainstorming, this simpler method brings a group of people together and presents them with a range of alternative solutions to a problem. They are then asked to choose what they see as the 'right' solution. This choice is made individually and without any debate or discussion, though questions may be asked about the factual content of the alternatives. The individual choices are not discussed or disclosed to the rest of the group but are written down on pieces of paper which are handed in to a group chairperson. This person will collate the group's choices and then tell the group which alternative received the lowest number of 'votes'. This alternative is then discarded and the process is repeated until a clear preference with a significant majority emerges. The process enables the:

- skills
- abilities
- intuition

of the group to be used, without the difficulties and pressures which, as we saw in Chapter 7, can generate a 'group think' solution.

155

> ❧ *Pause for reflection* ❧
> **Use the Delphi method to evaluate the alternatives that came from your brainstorming session.**

Ranking

We saw in Chapter 3 how the ranking method can be used to choose which of the alternative projects is to be implemented. Ranking can also be used to choose which of the alternative solutions is used to solve our project problem. As we saw, the ranking method is based upon the ordering, relative to each other, of these alternatives under a number of headings. The alternative with the best total ranking is then chosen for implementation. The headings chosen will reflect the:

■ stage of the project
■ nature of the problem

but must be equally applicable to all of the alternatives. In the early stages of the project it may be that the alternative with the shortest implementation time will be given preference, while at the later stages the nature and quality of the outcome will have a stronger influence on the choice made. An example of the use of weighted ranking to choose between alternative solutions is given in the table below.

Heading	Alternative solutions							
	A		B		C		D	
	Orig.	Wt'd	Orig.	Wt'd	Orig.	Wt'd	Orig.	Wt'd
Cost Weighting factor = 1	1	1	3	3	2	2	4	4
Time Weighting factor = 0.5	2	1	1	0.5	3	1.5	4	2
Outcome performance Weighting factor = 2	1	2	3	6	2	4	4	8
Outcome quality Weighting factor = 0.75	2	1.5	1	0.75	4	3	3	2.25
Totals		5.5		10.25		10.5		16.25

Weighted ranking

In this example, which uses a ranking scale in which 1 = best and 4 = worst, alternative A generates the lowest total weighted score and would therefore be adopted.

Summary

■ *Problems are situations which are:*
  - *not as we desire*
  - *difficult or troublesome*
  - *puzzling or perplexing*
  - *apparently insoluble.*

■ *Projects have problems which:*
  - *can be about any aspect of the project*
  - *can have a wide range of possible causes and an equally wide range of solutions.*

■ *Project problems are solved by:*
  - *collecting and analysing information*
  - *identifying the real problem*
  - *generating alternative solutions*
  - *choosing which alternative to implement.*

■ *Information on project problems can be:*
  - *collected by diagramming, sampling or ratioing*
  - *analysed by using averages, medians or modes, moving averages, or decision trees.*

■ *Alternative solutions can be:*
  - *generated by brainstorming or lateral thinking*
  - *evaluated by the Delphi method or ranking.*

157

11

Project conflicts

Overview

A project can involve many individuals and groups of people and the ambitions, hopes, needs and desires of those people are often incompatible with each other. These differences can lead to conflict and this chapter looks at the ways in which that conflict can be managed and yet still contribute to the success of the project.

Objectives

When you have read this chapter you should have a better under-standing of:
- the what and why of conflict
- the particular nature of project conflicts
- the ways in which those conflicts can be resolved
- the value of negotiation as a method of resolving conflict
- the skills required in order to negotiate effectively
- how effective negotiation can contribute to the success of the project.

Trouble and strife

We have already seen (Chapter 7) how an effective and efficient project team is a key factor in the success of any project and how the members of that team:

- share goals and purposes
- undertake co-operative action
- generate collective rather than individual outcomes.

And yet our own experiences will tell us that this is not always so and that people often have disagreements, rows and even fights because they hold differing views about what has been or ought to be done.

When these conflicts surface, as they do quite often, the ways in which our organisations react to and deal with them can differ widely. For example, in many organisations these conflicts are seen as:

- difficult
- troublesome
- embarrassing.

In short, an unwanted intrusion in the calm progression of ordered affairs. In such organisations these conflicts are 'managed' in ways which attempt to hide or suppress them or, as the ultimate sanction, purge them and their causes from the organisation.

But this response to conflict is not universal and many organisations use conflict creatively. A typical example of this use of conflict often occurs when managing the change process, and we saw in Chapter 9 that the effective manager of change:

- accepts that change and conflict go hand in hand
- uses that conflict constructively.

159

As we see from the world around us the presence of conflict in human affairs, in one form or another, is not unusual. This potential for conflict appears to be an ongoing feature of our relationships with one another – possibly because of the nature of the human animal with its innate drives to acquire territory and resources – and the ways in which we manage it in our workplaces and particularly in our projects can be key to our success.

We have already seen, in the examples given above, two radically different ways of managing conflict, and the question we must now answer is which of these or other ways is correct and which will help us to achieve success in our projects? In order to begin to answer that question we have to first look at the what and why of conflict and then examine the alternative ways in which that conflict can be managed.

Conflict – roots and causes

Conflict springs into existence when any one of us feels or thinks that others have frustrated, thwarted or foiled our interests or concerns, or intend to do so. These conflicts can be about any aspect of our affairs, and the diversity of their nature is such that they can be:

- short lived or long lasting
- between individuals or groups.

They might have consequences which are:

- minor or major
- short-lived or long lasting.

These conflicts occur because of the ways in which we behave towards one another, and typical examples embrace issues such as:

- **politics** – as with socialists and conservatives
- **religion** – as with Catholics and Protestants
- **sport** – as with supporters of Manchester United and Manchester City football teams
- **money** – who owes what to whom and when?

While these conflicts occur because of the differences between us, they can also occur because:

- limited resources are desired by several people or groups
- people are unsure about who is responsible for or supposed to do what
- rewards are seen to be unequal or unfair
- differing views or policies exist
- ' them and us' views are held
- people don't like or get on with each other.

> *≥ Pause for reflection ≥*
>
> **What sort of conflicts are common in your organisation?**
> **What are they about?**

Conflict – good or bad ?

The traditional view of conflict is that it is bad or even dysfunctional, i.e. involving abnormal or aberrant behaviour, and that it should be managed in ways that are targeted at limiting its effects on the people involved. But is this always so?

There are, of course, some forms or expressions of conflict such as wars, beating up old people or abusing children that are seen by all of us as unacceptable and 'bad'. But there are also other forms of conflict which result in new and better ways of doing things and greater understanding of our differences, and are seen as having 'good' outcomes.

Whether we see conflict to be 'good' or 'bad' is important as it will make a major difference to the ways in which we manage it.

If, for example, we see conflict as 'bad' then we might:

- avoid situations in which it might occur
- select project team members because they 'get on' with the rest of the team
- always give people who shout what they want.

But, in contrast, if we see conflict as 'good' then we might:

- be drawn to or even create situations in which friction and difficulties abound
- choose project team members because of the tensions and difficulties between them.

In fact, contrary to popular opinion, conflict has both good and bad sides. It can, for example:

- cause problems to be brought out into the open and hence solved
- cause groups to close ranks against a common enemy, with increased group loyalty
- encourage consideration of new ways of doing things
- increase the frequency and detail of our comparisons of our work performance with that of others, particularly those with whom we are in conflict
- motivate us to do better.

But it can also:

- stir up negative feelings and create stress, making workplaces unpleasant to be in
- interfere with communications between individuals and groups
- influence managers to shift towards a 'do as I tell you' style of leadership.

But our organisations are, above all, the arenas in which we play out our different needs, aims and desires and in which we struggle to find the balance between these individual hopes and desires and those of our employers. As such they represent and present situations and circumstances in which conflict is inevitable. They also, more often than not, present situations in which the choice is *not* one between 'good' conflict or 'bad' conflict but one which lies between too much conflict or too little conflict. If we have too much conflict in the workplace then productive effort will be wasted and high staff turnover might occur. On the other hand, too little conflict can encourage smugness, apathy, complacency and lethargy, none of which will help an organisation to survive the 1990s and none of which will lead to success in our projects.

❦ *Pause for reflection* ❦

Does your work team have:
good, healthy conflict or bad, destructive conflict
or
too much conflict or not enough conflict?

Projects and conflict

We have already seen in Chapter 4 that conflict is present in our projects and that it often occurs because of the opposing needs of the:

- client organisation
- project
- project team.

But what are these conflicts and when do they occur ?

The answer to that question is rarely a straightforward and simple one but, as we saw earlier, these project conflicts can occur because the client wants to be able to:

- influence the fine detail of project decisions
- have the freedom to change or modify the objectives of the project as and when required
- have a project team which owes allegiance to him or her.

The project however needs clear, unambiguous and specific objectives which are frozen or fixed at the earliest opportunity, and the project team needs:

- a project manager with clear and unconditional authority
- members who owe allegiance to the project
- the freedom to make decisions without outside interference.

These conflicts often spring up around such issues as:

- **plans and schedules** – who does what and when?
- **priorities** – what is done first and why?
- **technical matters** – do we use this or that?

162

- **administrative procedures** – whose accounting system do we use?
- **cost estimates and monitoring** – it can't have cost that much!
- **personalities** – can't stand the man!

While all of these typical conflicts will occur at all stages of the project life cycle the balance between them and their relative importance will change as the project moves from conception to birth and development into adulthood, and finally to old age and termination. For example, the adulthood stage is usually characterised by conflicts about:

- the differences between what was planned and what was achieved and how these can be solved
- how to solve emerging technical problems
- what are the priorities for allocation of people and other scarce resources.

On the other hand the old age and terminal stage will display conflicts about:

- the allocation of resources to ensure completion
- the relocation of the project team
- the handover of the completed project outcome to the client.

163

All in all, while these conflicts may differ both in the ways in which they are presented and their relative importance, they all, at their core, have issues about:

- influence
- authority
- autonomy.

As we noted before, the ways in which these conflicts are or are not resolved exert a considerable influence on the project's potential for success. We have also seen that at least part of the way in which these conflicts can be resolved lies in the way in which the project is organised. But, as we will now see, that is not the only solution to the dilemma presented by the often opposing needs of:

- the client organisation
- the project
- the project team.

Managing conflict

Conflict can be managed in a number of ways and the variety of these styles of conflict management reflects not only the wide ranging nature and causes of conflict but also the rich diversity of the ways in which we behave. Conflict can, for example, be managed by:

- **avoiding it:**
  - ignoring it and hoping it will go away
  - imposing a third party solution
  - imposing a blanket of 'secrecy'
  - imposing rules or procedures
- **dispersing or defusing it:**
  - behaving in smoothing ways, as in pouring oil on troubled waters
  - invoking a larger and more important goal so that the conflict diminishes in importance.
- **containing it:**
  - using somebody else to either arbitrate or represent those in conflict
  - negotiating or bargaining
- **confronting it:**
  - using joint problem solving or redesign situations.

164

The style that we choose to manage our conflicts will be influenced by and be dependent upon the circumstances in which it occurs. For example, a manager who is under pressure about goals or project milestone achievement may choose to manage a conflict by deferring action or buying time by using one of the avoidance styles. However, under other circumstances, it may be appropriate to confront the issues and people involved and spend time hammering out a solution. While we all have our own preferred style for handling conflict each of the above styles of conflict management will be appropriate at one time or another. Nevertheless, choosing the appropriate style requires skill and knowledge as it affects not only the results gained but also the longer term patterns of how we work together. A good project manager is one who accepts the inevitability of conflict and manages it in such a way as to energise the project and generate situations in which people are:

- willing to take risks
- able and willing to tell others how they feel.

A bad project manager is one who continually ignores or even suppresses conflict, thus de-energising the project and creating situations in which people are:

- unwilling to trust
- unwilling to be open with each other
- frustrated.

Our own experience tells us that, whatever the quality of the management or the style of conflict management chosen, these conflicts need to be resolved if our projects are to be successful. Unresolved conflicts act in ways which not only limit the commitment of the project team members but also divert energy away from the project goals and into areas of activity which are about 'getting even' rather than working co-operatively together. But as managers or as those who are managed we can still, as individuals, make choices about how we respond to conflict situations. One way of describing these choices is that of the win-lose matrix as shown below.

Individual or group B

		Win	Lose
Individual or group A	Win	Win–win	Win–lose
	Lose	Lose–win	Lose–lose

Win – lose matrix

This matrix tells us that when we are faced with a conflict with another individual or group we can choose to act:

- reactively, responding with equal or greater ferocity to the attacks of the other and allowing the level of conflict to escalate, with the result that we and the other both lose – a lose-lose result
- aggressively, aiming to overcome or defeat the other, with the result that we win and the other loses – a win-lose result
- passively, but aiming to minimise our losses, with the result that the other wins and we lose – a lose-win result
- assertively, without dominating the other but standing up for our 'rights' and willing to accept compromise, with the result that both we and the other win – a win-win result.

From all these choices, common sense and self protection generally lead us to prefer acting in ways which result in us achieving:

165

- **a win-lose result** *or*
- **a win-win result.**

While both of these conflict management outcomes are effective in the short term, only the win-win result will, in the long term, produce the sort of conflict management outcomes which lead to project success. Win-win results lead to increased trust and commitment and enable future outcomes to be built on the firm foundations of past successes, while winning, because others lose, will result in them redoubling their efforts to win next time – when you will lose. One of the most powerful and effective ways of achieving that win-win outcome is by the use of negotiating or bargaining.

Negotiating and bargaining

When we think about the acts of negotiating and bargaining many pictures and memories may spring to mind. We may, for example, think of unions and companies locked in conflict over wage rates or we may recall the TV pictures of American and Russian presidents negotiating over nuclear arms reductions. At a more personal level we may remember the toing and froing that took place when we bought our last house or the long drawn out haggling process that finished with our purchase of an overpriced rug in the bazaar at Fez. All of these are examples of the process that is often called negotiating or bargaining – a process used by all of us and integral to the fabric of our lives. At home we may, for example, negotiate about what we have for dinner, whether we go out this evening and to do what, who does the washing up and who does the dusting. In the workplace our negotiations may be concerned about when we finish that report that the boss wants, what priority we allocate to our many tasks or who is on duty over the weekend.

These negotiations may be conducted:

- by two people on a one to one basis
- by groups of people.

They can be undertaken in:

- a formal way
- an informal manner

and can involve people who:

- are directly concerned with or involved in the issues being discussed
- are representatives of those involved.

In our projects, negotiations can be about such issues as:

- when activities will be undertaken
- who will do them
- at what cost they will be done.

But our project negotiations may also result from more significant and far reaching proposals for change or modification to the project specification. As such these negotiations will involve issues such as:

- what extra cost will be incurred
- what additional time is needed
- what are the implications for the quality of the project outcome.

If we are to use this process of negotiation effectively then we must recognise that it has conflict as its starting point and its *raison d'être*. Without this conflict – the difference between what we want and what others desire – there would be no reason to negotiate and no issues over which to bargain. The process of negotiation starts from that difference and aims to:

- identify areas of potential agreement
- convert that potential into concrete reality

and to do so by generating outcomes which are acceptable to all.

Negotiating is often seen as a win-lose process, such as when we buy our Moroccan rug at a price which we think is well below its real value or when we sell our house at a price which is more than we had hoped for, without telling the buyers about the stains behind the cupboard. But if our negotiations are to contribute to the success of our projects then they must be aimed at both sides winning – a win-win process – and so be based upon collaboration rather than competition and trust rather than evasion and concealment.

Negotiating – the ways and means

The process of negotiating has, at its heart, the simple act of bargaining. We bargain when we want to trade, buy or sell goods or services in exchange for money. This act, which has its roots far back in the history of humankind, is different to that of bartering, which involves exchanging goods or services for other goods or services. It involves, in its simplest form, two people in face to face discussion aimed at trying to find out if they can agree on a price or value. But when we think further about the act of bargaining we begin to realise that there is not just one unique price which may or may not be found. The buyer, for example, will have a cost which he or she is not pre-pared to exceed and another lower cost that he or she hopes to achieve. The seller will also have two prices – the one below which he or she is not prepared to sell and the another that represents the price at which he or she hopes to sell. On further reflection we may also realise that the buyer and seller open the process of negotiation with the first of a series of offers and counter offers. The buyer will offer to buy at a very low cost and the seller will counter with a very high offer to sell. The high and low levels of these offers are aimed to give both buyer and seller the opportunity to move towards each other in price or cost terms and, in so doing, appear to be compromis-ing. In win-lose negotiations the buyer will attempt to pull the seller's price offers down – if possible to the level of the buyer's 'hoped for' cost – while the seller will attempt to push the buyer's cost offers up – again if possible to the level of the seller's 'hoped for' price. These price and cost levels can be illustrated as shown below.

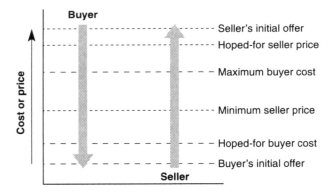

The offer spectrum

The dodging and ducking and weaving that goes on during this offer and counter offer sequence will include such routines as:

- giving ground slowly and reluctantly
- making threats
- invoking company policy

- saying that there is nothing left to give
- imposing deadlines
- consulting outsiders.

Factors which will influence the final equilibrium position for this push and pull process include:

- how skilled and experienced the negotiators are
- the presence or absence of alternative sellers and buyers
- previous price levels

and, as it is often a win-lose negotiation:

- who won or lost last time.

The bargaining zone

When we look more closely at the various costs and prices shown in the previous diagram we begin to see that they also define a zone or area in which there may exist a compromise or win-win solution to the conflict between the opposing needs of the seller and the buyer.

169

This zone or area, which is often called the bargaining zone, has as its upper and lower boundaries:

- the minimum seller price
- the maximum buyer cost

and can be illustrated by the diagram below.

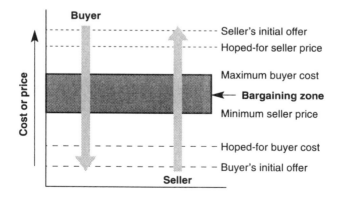

The bargaining zone

To enter this zone and achieve a successful win-win outcome requires real skill and commitment on the part of both negotiators. It also requires the effective use of a wide range of skills, which include the ability to:

- build a relationship with the other negotiator that contains a strong element of mutual trust
- quickly and accurately identify what is happening in the negotiations
- recognise why it is happening
- decide what to do about it
- communicate with clarity and precision about:
- facts
- feelings
- impressions
- listen without bias or prejudice.

Use the following questionnaire to check out your negotiating ability.

170

HOW GOOD A NEGOTIATOR ARE YOU?

Under each of the headings below ring a number which is nearest to the way that you manage your projects and then add up your total.

1 Aims and objectives

I always aim to get the best deal for my side.	1 2 3 4 5 6 7	I try to get a deal which is good for everyone.

2 Communication

I say things in my way and hope they'll understand.	1 2 3 4 5 6 7	I try to reach the other negotiator.
I hide my feelings and keep a poker face.	1 2 3 4 5 6 7	I share my impressions and show my feelings.

3 Preparation

I just turn up and play it 'off the cuff'.	1 2 3 4 5 6 7	I prepare what I want to do and why.

4 Process

I make sure that I'm in control.	1 2 3 4 5 6 7	I watch what's happening and respond to the other negotiator's moves.

I never make a concession.	1 2 3 4 5 6 7	I often make concessions.

Key:

Total

6–18   Next time you may not be so lucky!

19–30   Well done – use your low scores to identify where you need to negotiate better.

31–42   You've obviously done this before – keep it up.

In order to use these skills effectively the skilled negotiator will, before the negotiation, have:

- made sure that he or she has talked and listened to, read, observed and digested *all* of the information sources relevant to the negotiation
- thought through and prepared a generalised campaign plan or strategy
- decided what are the levels of his or her:
  - hoped for cost or price
  - minimum cost or maximum price
  - initial offer
- decided what the escape plan will be if the hoped for win-win negotiation turns out to be a lose-win one.

Project managers and negotiations

The project manager is involved in negotiations throughout every stage of the project's life cycle and the presence and use of real skill, experience and knowledge in those negotiations can make a considerable difference to the ways in which the project is conducted. In the earliest stage of the project's conception these negotiations are concerned with creating order out of uncertainty, and even chaos, and will focus on issues such as:

- defining the project's objectives
- deciding the form of the project's organisation
- making sure adequate resources are available.

As the project progresses to its birth and development stage the focus of these negotiations will shift from the 'broad brush' generalities of the previous stage to the fine detail and specifics of the plans, programmes and procedures which must now be created. These negotiations may be concerned with:

- technical issues – over which the project manager may have limited authority (or expertise) but which can significantly affect the project budget and time-scale
- pledges and promises of future support – as in a client-focused project organisation in which the project manager is reliant upon other departments for his team members, or as in relationships with contractors.

The negotiations of the project manager during the adulthood stage of the project are generally concerned with bridging the gap between the detail of the planned objectives for the project and the reality of what has been achieved. Even in the best of projects, plans will go wrong and milestones will be missed, and the project manager's negotiating skills will then be focused on getting the project back on the rails by:

- generating agreement to new or revised priorities
- gaining everybody's commitment to those new targets
- ensuring adequate resources are available to meet the new targets.

During the final and terminal stage of the project the project manager's negotiations will be about:

- the detail of the handover to the client
- targets for the completion of the client's list of minor items needing corrective action
- the relocation of project staff.

The quality of both the outcomes *and* the content of all of the project manager's negotiations are significant to the success of the project. The outcomes of these negotiations are important in terms of the skills, experience and resources made available to the project. The content of these negotiations and particularly the presence (or absence) of mutual trust and joint commitment to the project which will have built up during these negotiations will spread beyond the negotiating room and into the main body of the project, thus creating (or destroying) a genuine team environment with a shared will to succeed.

Summary

- *Conflict occurs in all of our organisations and in all of our projects.*
- *The effects of conflict are both good and bad.*
- *Project conflicts are about the often opposing interests and needs of:*
  - *the client*
  - *the project*
  - *the project team.*
- *At their core these conflicts have the issues of:*
  - *influence*
  - *authority*
  - *autonomy.*
- *Conflicts need to be resolved and managed.*
- *This can be done by:*
  - *avoidance or dispersion/defusion*
  - *containment or confrontation.*
- *The choice of conflict management style depends upon:*
  - *circumstance*
  - *context*
  - *preference.*
- *Accepting and managing conflict leads to:*
  - *increased trust and risk taking*
  - *win-win situations.*
- *Ignoring or suppressing conflict generates:*
  - *low levels of trust and openness*
  - *frustration*
  - *lose-win, win-lose or lose-lose situations.*
- *Negotiations can be used to achieve win-win situations.*
- *Negotiations occur throughout the whole of the project life cycle.*
- *Effective negotiations require skill and ability.*

173

12
Project monitoring and control

Overview

The conduct and passage of our projects are often strongly influenced by the volatility and unpredictability of the real world. For this reason, their journeys from beginning to end are rarely as straight and true as we plan them to be and, from time to time, action needs to be taken to bring them back to the original planned course. This chapter looks at the ways in which the progress of a project can be monitored and controlled and how these can contribute to the success of that project.

Objectives

By reading this chapter you should gain an understanding of the ways in which the progress of all projects can be:
- **measured**
- **monitored**
- **compared to its goals and targets**
- **controlled.**

Bridging the gap

In earlier chapters we have looked at the ways in which we convert our project outcomes from the broad concepts of the project's early life to the precision and detail of the project specification. We have also seen how that specification is then converted into a project plan – a sequence of intended actions that gives life and form to our desire to reach out and control the future of the project. But things don't always happen in the ways that we plan them to. The material deliveries of our project can be delayed, key project activities can run into unforeseen snags and difficulties and fail to achieve their scheduled completion dates, and equipment can break down just when we need it for a critical path task. When any of these or other similar calamities occur the net result is to put at risk our ability to create the outcomes of our project:

- at the right time
- with the desired performance
- at the right cost
- with the desired quality.

What we need, under these all too common circumstances, is a quick and efficient system which will:

- tell us when things are not as they ought to be
- enable us to correct or limit the effects of that difference.

The first of these needs is answered by the process of monitoring – a process which involves the activities of:

- measuring
- collecting
- recording
- collating
- analysing

information about any or all of the aspects of the project and then comparing that information to the targets and planned achievements of the project. The results of these activities should, if they are to be effective, provide the project manager with the answers to such key questions as:

- will we finish on time?
- will we achieve what we set out to do?
- will we overspend the budget?

The answers should also tell the project manager:

- what the gaps or differences are between the actual and the planned performance of the project
- where, in the project's many activities and tasks, these differences are occurring
- when they started to occur.

The second need is to be able to do something about these differences when they do occur – as it were to bridge the gap between the project plan and reality – and to do so in a manner which is both timely and effective.

Whatever actions we take to bridge this gap, their outcomes should result in a reduced or even eliminated difference between the project plan and the reality of the real world. These actions make up the process of control – a process which feeds on the information provided by the process of monitoring and enables the project manager to manage the progress of the project and take the actions necessary to ensure that it achieves its planned performance, cost, duration and quality. The twin processes of monitoring and control are key to the success of our project, but, as is the case with all such closed related mechanisms, their outcomes and actions must be closely integrated if they are to be effective in their contribution to that success. What we will do now is to look at each of them in turn and in so doing examine how, when integrated, they contribute to the success of our projects.

Monitoring

As we saw earlier in this chapter, monitoring our projects involves us in the actions of:

- measuring or testing their performance
- converting the data gathered into meaningful forms.

But this is not an academic or intellectual exercise, for all of this is undertaken solely that we might know more about what is happening on the project. However, if this monitoring is to be effective in its contribution to the success of our project, we must first take the initial step of deciding:

- what we are to monitor
- how often we are to do so.

This is a key step which determines not only the value of our monitoring but also the nature of that process's contribution to the success of our project. If, for example, we decide to monitor too many aspects of our project then our ability to see and react to deviations from our project plan will be limited by:

- too large a volume of information
- the time it takes to analyse that information.

If, however, we monitor too few of these aspects then we might miss the drift or movement of another key aspect, and not be able to react until it is too late. We must also choose what we monitor with care and not in an indiscriminate way, and we must focus the attention of our monitoring process upon those aspects of the project which are key to the project success. Obviously, these aspects must tell us about the key dimensions of our project:

- performance
- cost
- time
- quality.

But what aspect or feature of these dimensions will we actually measure and how often?

The enormous variety of our projects and their outcomes makes it impossible to answer this question in a detailed and specific way and, in any case, that decision ultimately lies with the managers of each project. However, there are a number of basic and general rules which, if followed, will enable the monitoring process to contribute to the success of the project. These rules tell us that we should focus on the measurement and monitoring of aspects of the project which are:

177

- measured easily
- timely
- easily understood
- credible
- relevant.

For example, when we apply these rules to a project where the cost is dominated by its labour costs we will find that it is easier and quicker to monitor the weekly totals of labour hours logged rather than wait for the monthly invoices for labour costs. Similarly, these rules will guide us to monitor project factors such as:

- length of cable laid
- number of words written
- area of carpet laid

for projects in which these are relevant and credible. But, of course, our monitoring isn't limited to these 'quick and easy' factors any more than a doctor will base a diagnosis of a patient's health on pulse rate alone. We need to be able to link our monitored project aspects back to those two core expressions of the project:

- the project plan
- the project budget.

> *❧ Pause for reflection ❧*
> **Look at a project and decide whether you
> monitor what is happening and when.**

Monitoring the project plan

We saw in Chapter 5 that the project plan is about the actions of the project and as such it tells us:

- when those actions are to be done
- who is to do them
- what equipment, tools, etc. we need to do them.

Nevertheless, however sophisticated or detailed this plan might be, it is still only a statement of our intentions and desires or, to put it another way, what we want to happen in our project. As the project progresses we will inevitably find that events don't turn out as we had hoped or planned, and this may force us to deviate from or even to change the plan. It is this interaction between the actuality of real events and the intentions of the plan that we need to monitor if our projects are to be successful. In order to do that we have to accept that our plans are more than just paper models of an unrealistic future or convincing wall decorations – we have to accept that our project plans are tools which are:

- meaningful
- usable
- easily understood
- capable of change.

For many tyro project managers this is a difficult step – after all, a plan is a plan and if you don't mean to follow it why bother to create it in the first place? But a plan, if it is to contribute to the success of our project, must be seen to be and must be used as a tool, an instrument of management, a means of effecting the outcomes of our project and, since our projects are about change, the plan itself must also be capable of change. That process of identifying and implementing change is one of the ways in which we control our project – a process that we shall look at later in this chapter and one which, as we saw earlier, must always be preceded by the process of monitoring. When

178

we use our plans to monitor and record the progress of our project we do that by comparing the achieved with the intended, and as we saw in Chapter 5 this can be done:

- graphically – as in the filled in bars of the Gantt chart
- numerically – as in the data recorded on the nodes of the AON or the arrows of the AOA networks.

Milestones or tombstones?

We can also record and compare the progress of our project by the use of what are often called the project milestones. These are events which we can use to mark our progress through the various stages of a project's growth and decline, and as such must be:

- clearly identifiable
- significant
- on the project's critical path.

They can represent the:

- end of a sequence of activities – such as those associated with the creation of a house's foundations
- the beginning of a sequence of activities – such as the acceptance, by the publisher, of the writer's manuscript for a book, which then begins a sequence of activities associated with editing and printing.

These milestones can be indicated:

- graphically – as in the unfilled (scheduled) or filled (completed) diamonds of the typical Gantt chart
- with the words and dates of a milestone report – as in:

Milestone no.	Scheduled date	Achieved date
1	25/10/95	24/10/95

The use of milestones as a tool for monitoring the status of projects provides us with feedback which enables us to quickly and easily understand that status and so begin the process of managing and controlling that project on its road to success.

Beyond the limits

Another technique that we can use to assess the status of our projects involves the use of what is often called limit testing. This involves:

- measuring some aspect of the project
- comparing the measured value with a preset level
- acting only if and when this limit is exceeded.

This process, which is sometimes also called go-no go testing, can be applied to any aspect of the project. It can, for example, be used to monitor:

- project spend
- project activity rates
- project milestone achievement.

This technique can be:

- easily integrated into existing information systems
- operated by any member of the project team
- operated manually or by use of computers.

Limit testing also makes effective use of the project manager's time since he or she is involved only when the preset limit has been exceeded. The responses and actions which are triggered when this limit is exceeded can be adjusted to be relevant to the level of the limit. For example, if we are monitoring weekly project spend levels our preset limits and responses might be as follows:

Preset Limit	Action
Budget plus 5%	Investigate cause
Budget plus 10%	Initiate initial cost control actions
Budget plus 20%	Reduce cost by:
	– stopping non-critical activities
	– reducing other activity rates

We can also use preset levels to trigger:

- increased (or reduced) frequency of reporting
- reduced (or increased) labour levels.

Go-no go testing can also be used to trigger consequential actions and activities as, for example, when, on reaching a project milestone, we:

- start work on the activities leading to the next project milestone
- call a project progress review or planning meeting
- issue a formal project progress report.

In short, we can use limit or go-no go testing to:

- bring the progress of critical areas of the project to our attention
- enable us to manage our projects in ways which will use our skills and abilities more effectively.

❧ Pause for reflection ❧

Review the preset limits that you would set for a critical path activity and how you would respond when they were exceeded.

Monitoring the money

181

We saw in Chapter 8 that the project budget plays an important role in the management of all our projects and enables the project manager to see:

- what money is needed
- when it is needed.

We can also use that budget to monitor the spend of the project and to give us information about how and when we need to adjust or modify its cash flow. One of the ways in which we can do this is by the use of what is often called the S curve, as illustrated below.

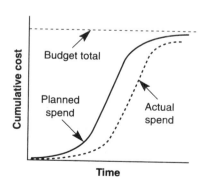

The S curve

This curve shows us the budgeted pattern of project spend and enables us to compare this with the actual spend. But the actual spend, which is recorded in our project accounts, may be below (or above) the budgeted spend because:

■ the work completed cost less (or more) than we planned
■ or we have completed less work than planned – but at a greater cost.

The differences between these are very significant – on the one hand we have a situation in which our future costs are likely to be below the budgeted level while on the other hand our future costs are likely to exceed that level. But how do we tell which is likely to happen? One of the ways in which we can solve this conundrum is to introduce the idea of earned value analysis (EVA). This way of looking at project costs suggests that we monitor them by:

■ measuring the units of work actually done
■ multiplying this by the unit cost used in the budget, which gives us the budgeted cost of work performed (BCWP)
■ comparing this to the actual cost of this work (ACWP) and the budgeted cost of the work that we had planned to do, or the budgeted cost of work scheduled (BCWS).

The differences between these figures will tell us:

■ the difference between the budgeted value of the work performed and the actual cost of that work. This is called the cost variance (CV) and is equal to (BCWP – ACWP)
■ the difference between the budgeted value of the work performed and the budgeted value of the work that we had planned to perform. This is called the schedule variance (SV) and is equal to (BCWP – BCWS).

These variances will tell us, for example, whether the differences in cost shown by the S curve are due to:

■ the actual unit cost being higher than budgeted unit costs – as would be shown if the CV was negative, i.e. BCWP < ACWP
■ achieving less than we planned to do – as would be shown if the SV was negative, i.e. BCWP < BCWS.

This information will then, as we will see later in this chapter, enable the project manager to decide what actions are required to bring the costs of the project back under control and on course.

Progress reports

The progress of our project can also be recorded and compared to its plan by the use of project progress reports. These can be:

■ regular – as in once a month
■ special – such as when problems occur or significant events like milestones have occurred.

The progress report can be used to:

■ gather data which is then collated and reported in a larger report
■ to record information for future use
■ to communicate information to the client and other interested parties.

A typical medium-to-large project would, for example, have regular progress reports from:

■ specialist functions – such as the software programmers, structural engineers, trainers or computer specialists
■ the project team – reporting to their colleagues and the project manager
■ the project manager – reporting progress and milestone completion to the client.

This project may also have a number of special reports which are issued as and when required and might be concerned with such issues as:

■ debugging a key software routine
■ solving welding problems
■ identifying the causes of a delay in the completion of a key activity.

The regular reports which the project manager presents to the client represent an important strand in the communications between them, and is one which can be a major contributor to the quality of that relationship and hence to the success of the project. All or any of these reports can also make an important contribution to the quality of our project monitoring process. However, in order to do that they have to be:

■ understandable
■ concise
■ based on facts rather than opinions.

The structure and frequency of these reports will, of course, depend upon their purpose. In general, brevity is not only desirable but also

183

necessary if the report is to be read and understood by the busy reader. For this reason, supporting data, where required, should be nested in appendices, and a condensed version of the report's conclusions and recommendations should be contained in an up-front summary. The writer of a short report will often adopt the following structure:

1 Title
2 Summary
3 Background and introduction
4 Findings
5 Recommendations

while the project's routine progress report might consist solely of tables of figures, Gantt charts or AOA networks, with little or no written or analytical comment. Whatever their structure, these reports are often issued to coincide with the occurrence of the next method of monitoring project progress that we shall look at – the project meeting.

The project meeting

Meetings are important. But, as many of you will have experienced, meetings are often formal, ritualised and time wasting events which are organised and implemented in order to:

■ define or confirm the status of those who attend
■ exert pressure on others to conform to group norms
■ reinforce group beliefs
and, occasionally, to communicate.

The meetings of successful projects are, however, not the time wasting, status reinforcing events to which so many managers have become accustomed. They are gatherings where the purpose is to contribute to the effective and efficient conduct of the project and, as such, they are focused towards the achievement of:

■ results
■ targets.

These meetings are a key element in the processes of monitoring and controlling the progress of our projects, and their objectives include:

■ the exchange of factual information
■ the exchange of opinions, views and feelings
■ the support of the project manager's decision making process.

As we saw in Chapter 6, in order to reach the objectives in an effective and effective manner these meetings must be:

- chaired by the project manager
- have agendas and minutes
- be attended by no more than ten participants
- involve participants who have:
- relevant functional skills and knowledge
- adequate interpersonal skills
- have a duration no longer than 1.5 hours.

The chairperson role in all meetings, and particularly project meetings, is a role which can make or break the effectiveness of that meeting. Effective chairpeople are concerned with the regulation of the meeting's proceedings rather than advocating or representing a particular line or policy. This can often present difficulties for project managers who are, after all, responsible for the conduct and completion of the project. But projects are rarely conducted or managed by project managers acting as solo or sole agents and the delegation, by the project manager, of that advocacy to other members of the project team will often contribute more in net terms than the eclipsing of the project meeting by the project manager. The documents of project meetings will consist of:

- **an agenda** – issued well before the meeting and telling meeting participants:
  - when and where the meeting is to be held
  - what subjects are to be discussed
  - in what order they will be discussed.
- **reports** – again issued well before the meeting and containing detail on relevant aspects of the project or its problems
- **minutes** – issued after the meeting and providing a record of:
  - what was decided
  - who is responsible for implementation
  - when implementation is due to be complete.

Project meetings should not be long drawn out affairs from which participants emerge tired and drawn, rather they should be, as we saw earlier, meetings which are focused on:

- results
- targets

and from which participants emerge with :

185

- decisions about key issues
- more and better information about the project
- a clear understanding of their own project role and responsibilities.

An effective project meeting is only as good as the people who participate in it and, if they are to contribute to the success of the project, these participants must be able to:

- speak with precision and clarity
- listen to others
- make judgements and decisions
- negotiate with others.

Given these participants and an experienced and capable chairperson, project meetings are capable of making a significant contribution to both the monitoring and the control of our projects.

186

> *≈ Pause for reflection ≈*
> **How do you run your project meetings?**

Controlling

We saw earlier in this chapter that, in addition to monitoring the progress of our projects, we also need to be able to do something about any activities or costs which differ from those of our plans, and do so in a manner which is both timely and effective. This, the process of controlling our projects, is intended to reduce or eliminate the differences between:

- what we planned should happen
- what is actually happening.

One way of looking at this process draws heavily on what is, not surprisingly, called control system theory. This tells us that we often control our systems by:

- measuring their output
- comparing this with a desired or target level
- if there is a difference, adjusting the input to the system in ways which are related to the size of that difference and whether the difference is negative or positive.

We can illustrate this process, which is called feedback control, as shown below:

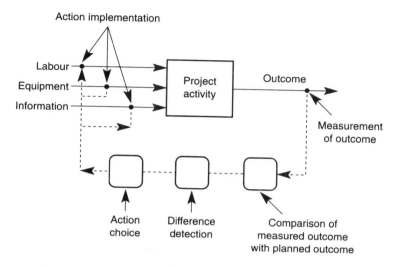

Feedback control

When we apply this process to, for example, the task of tiling the roof of a house, we would start by measuring the area of roof tiled per day. We would then compare the rate measured to the rate that we planned to achieve. If there was a difference between these we might find that the achieved rate is lower or higher than the planned rate.

If the difference between the achieved and planned rates was negative, i.e. the planned was greater than the achieved, then we would need to decide if we needed to increase the labour or equipment inputs by providing more people or faster or larger capacity equipment. If the reverse was evident and the achieved rate had exceeded the planned rate then we would need to decide whether we were going to:

■ reduce the number of people
■ provide lower capacity equipment
■ finish the task earlier than planned.

We might also find that the difference between these rates was large or small.

If the difference was small we might decide to do nothing, but increase our frequency of measurement so that we get rate figures every half day. However, when this difference was large we would have to do something, and we might again decide, when the achieved rate was lower than the planned, to:

- increase the number of people on the job
- get a tile lift.

If the achieved rate was considerably higher than the planned rate we might decide to:

- reduce the number of people on the job
- stop work on the roof for a few days, transferring the labour to other tasks which were not going as well
- find out why the tiling rate was high so that we could achieve the same high rate on other jobs.

188

All of these represent choices about what we are to do in order to reduce or increase the actual task performance to the level that we planned to achieve. But, as we saw in Chapters 6 and 10, we don't always have the information that we need. Despite our best intentions, the feedback on task performance might consist of information which is insufficient, inaccurate or out of date.

Under these circumstances the project manager will have to use some of the information gathering and analysis techniques that we looked at in Chapter 10. Examples of this will include the use of ratioing, which is already evident in our roof tiling example, or the use of sampling, at random times in the day, to increase the information that we have about tiling rates. The manner in which the project manager exerts this control is, as we saw in Chapter 6, dependent upon a number of factors, including:

- the project nature and its constraints, such as time, money, etc.
- the prior experience and relationship of the project manager and team.

However, the style or manner in which this process of project control takes place must:

- be based on information rather than opinions
- take into account the needs and presence of the project's people
- be targeted towards the enhancement the project's performance.

Check out your monitoring and control by using the following questionnaire.

HOW GOOD ARE YOU AT PROJECT MONITORING AND CONTROL?

Under each of the headings below ring a number which is nearest to the way that you manage your projects and then add up your total.

1 Monitoring

I let things take their own course	1 2 3 4 5 6 7	I keep an eye on what's happening.
I measure everything.	1 2 3 4 5 6 7	I monitor the key aspects of the project.
I monitor the complex sophisticated aspects of the project.	1 2 3 4 5 6 7	I monitor easily understood, timely and relevant aspects.

2 Control

These things usually sort themselves out.	1 2 3 4 5 6 7	I need to monitor what's happening and react in a relevant manner.
I react in the same way every time.	1 2 3 4 5 6 7	My reactions are geared to what's happening.

Key:

Total

5–15   You seem to be having problems.

15–25   Well done – use your low scores to identify where you need to monitor and control better.

25–35   You've either done it before or aren't being honest.

Summary

■ *The effective and efficient use of the processes of monitoring and controlling is essential to project success.*

■ *Project monitoring involves:*
 - *measuring*
 - *collecting*
 - *recording*
 - *collating*
 - *analysing information.*

■ *Monitoring is based on:*
 - *the project plan*
 - *the project budget.*

■ *Monitoring can use:*
 - *project milestones*
 - *limit testing*
 - *S curves*
 - *earned value analysis*
 - *progress reports*
 - *project meetings.*

■ *Controlling the project is aimed at reducing the gap between what is happening and what we had planned should happen.*

■ *The successful project is controlled by:*
 - *measuring what is happening*
 - *comparing it to what should be happening*
 - *adjusting the project inputs in ways which reflect the size and polarity of the difference.*

13
Project closure

Overview

All projects come to an end and the ways in which the project 'last rites' are conducted is just as important to the success of the project as the ways in which it has been planned, started and managed. This chapter looks at the process of project closure and examines the ways in which it can contribute to the success of the project.

Objectives

By the end of this chapter you should have a better understanding of:
- **the problems of project closure**
- **the ways in which that closure can be undertaken**
- **the ways in which that process can ensure that the project performance is constructively and objectively evaluated**
- **the ways in which the lessons learnt, problems solved and techniques and tools developed can be recorded and passed on for use in other projects.**

At the end of the day

All projects come to a close – a final end-point – from which they pass into the history books. As we move towards that closure we progress through the excitement and rapid progress of the early stages of the project's life cycle, the achievements of the adulthood stage and the satisfaction of seeing the outcomes develop from small beginnings to their final form. Plans which were original and new are overtaken by actuality, and the freshness and zest of a new project team will have become blunted by familiarity. By the time we reach this, the final stage of the project life cycle, much of the work of the project will be about detail – dotting the i's and crossing the t's – and project team members will be looking forward to the challenge of the next project or returning to their old jobs. In many ways the end of a project presents more difficulties than its start. In the beginning all is new and the hopes and challenges of the future lie before us, while by the end we have achieved, for good or bad, what we were able to achieve and naught can be changed. But, despite both its place at the end of the project's life cycle and its focus on detail and departure, this final stage of a project still has the potential to contribute to the success of the project and still requires the skills and abilities of a competent project manager.

In this chapter we will look at:

■ the problems that arise in this stage
■ how these can be managed and solved in ways which contribute to the success of the project.

Terminal problems

While many of the problems that face us at the end of our project are concerned with detail, they are also concerned with the final phase of the change process which has been the *raison d'être* of our project. When we looked, in Chapter 9, at this change process what we saw was that effective change management was concerned with the ways in which we balanced and co-ordinated our use of:

■ information
■ communication
■ people
■ power.

Despite the major differences in pace and content between this final stage and the earlier stages of the project, the need to manage these aspects in a co-ordinated and effective manner still remains a key task for the project manager. In carrying out this task, the project manager will need to be aware that:

■ members of the project team will be:
  – concerned about their futures
  – losing interest in the remaining tasks
  – showing reduced levels of motivation
  – not as committed to the team as they were in earlier stages
■ the client will be:
  – showing less interest in the project at a senior level
  – not attending project meetings or not available when needed

- increasingly interested, at client operating staff level, in the details of the project outcomes
■ the project will need:
  - outstanding outcomes identified and completed
  - contracts and work orders closed
  - disposal of physical assets
  - historic data collated and analysed
  - warranties and guarantees implemented.

The project manager will also need to be aware that this task is being carried out under circumstances in which:

■ the authority of his or her role is shrinking
■ his or her acceptance by the client is lessening
■ the team is getting smaller.

And yet many project managers and project management textbooks view this stage of the project as being one which requires little care and attention and one which is characterised by the routine nature of its tasks. In fact, all of the above and other factors combine together to create a unique and demanding set of problems which require management skill of a high order if the project is to be finally successful.

193

> ### ꙮ *Pause for reflection* ꙮ
> **Do you plan the closure of your projects?**

What we now need to look at is the how, when and why of that process of managing the end of the project and we shall do that by looking, in turn, at each of the key aspects of:

■ people
■ communication
■ information
■ power.

Managing the people

We have already seen that all projects, whatever their outcomes, are people-centred and that they need, if they are to be successful, to be managed in ways which enable and empower those people. This applies to the final phase of the project just as much as it more obviously applies to the earlier and more active stages. But in this, the final project phase, the needs and concerns of the people involved begin to move out beyond the boundaries of the project and begin to focus on longer term issues. This means that project staff will become concerned with issues such as:

■ the fact that the project team is slowly but surely disbanding
■ which project will they work on next?
■ when will they leave this project team?
■ will they get their old jobs back?

and client staff will be concerned with issues such as:

■ when do we get to run it?
■ will it do what we want it to?
■ the next project
■ the need to get the project 'wrapped up and closed out'.

194

There may even be changes of personnel involved, with key experts on both sides being moved on to new projects which demand their skills and time. These changes may also include that of the project manager role where the previous incumbent may have left for greener pastures, leaving the job of 'tidying up the details' to a project team member who is less experienced or who may have previously occupied a junior role on that team.

All of these factors mean that the:

■ composition
■ ambience
■ tasks

of the project team are changing and change, as we saw in Chapter 9, is usually resisted by those who are involved in or exposed to it. In order to manage this situation effectively the project manager must make sure that both the project team and the client are:

■ encouraged to maintain their commitment to the project
■ encouraged to self-manage the definition and implementation of the remaining project tasks
■ provided with enough information and resources to ensure that those tasks can be completed.

One example of this process can be the creation and support of joint project team/client snag listing teams that are responsible for auditing the state of the project outcomes and identifying a jointly agreed list of outstanding work or defects. Another example will be the creation of joint plans for the transfer of the project outcome from the project manager to the client operations manager. This will require careful planning which must take into account the needs of both the parties involved.

The relocation or transfer of project team personnel often faces the project manager with particular difficulties. On the one hand, the project needs to maintain, even until its last gasp, an effective team of experienced personnel. On the other hand, project personnel need, and will only perform well if they have, some certainty about the continuity or location of their future employment. The project manager needs to manage this situation with care, taking into account both individual needs and the needs of the project. Block or mass departures and reassignments tend to leave project team members feeling that their individual needs are not taken into account and lead to limited commitment on the part of remaining project members. Sudden unannounced departures lead to anxiety on the part of both project team members and client personnel and leave an impression of unplanned and ad hoc reassignments. Time spent, by the project manager, in planning this team wind down – even to the point of involving team members in the creation of the reassignment plan – will pay dividends in terms of the commitment and performance of the remaining and departing team members. The need to ensure that this commitment is maintained, even in the face of diminishing teams, now leads us to look at the communication aspect of this project closure process.

195

Managing the communications

We already know that effective two-way communication is a vital ingredient of the complex mix that leads to project success, and this, the final stage of our project, is no exception to that rule. Indeed, it can be argued that the unique pressures and difficulties of this stage lead to an increased demand for effective communication. This demand, if not met, can lead to difficulties, misunderstandings and problems which make the project end-point a blurred, confused and prolonged affair rather than the sharp, clear and efficient event that it ought to be. Examples of areas in which this increased demand will demonstrate its presence will include when the client needs to:

- plan any training needed by his or her staff
- examine the need to adapt and modify procedures and systems
- plan for increased or different raw material or product storage
- plan press releases or publicity

and when the project manager needs to:

- plan the reassignment of staff
- ensure an orderly project close down
- gather all the information that is needed to ensure that the lessons learned and experience gained are recorded.

We have already seen that the successful project manager ensures that the commitment and enthusiasm of the people involved in the project are maintained and encouraged by delegation and the provision of adequate resources. Communication has its role in this process with information flowing between project manager, client and project team. For example, this communication might involve information and targets from the project manager and feedback on progress and findings from the joint project team/client snag listing teams. Communication is always a two-way process and the project manager and client decision makers will need to have access to each other in order to ensure that briefing and debriefing occur and that this, the final stage of the project, moves to an orderly conclusion.

The mechanisms for this communication will already exist. They are the project meetings and reports that, as we saw in Chapter 12, have been a regular and routine feature of the project's monitoring and control systems. During this final phase of the project it may be necessary to:

- hold these meetings more frequently
- extend the attendance to include :
- all of the members of the smaller project team
- client personnel involved in snag listing, commissioning, etc.
- allow the meeting to consider matters of detail that would previously not have been considered by this meeting.

The project manager will also hold meetings with his or her team at which team issues such as reassignments or changes in team member duties are discussed. However it is conducted, this process of communication is vital to the effective and efficient closure of the project. That process cannot, however, take place without information.

Managing the information

By the time we reach this final stage of the project:

- almost all of the money will have been spent or allocated
- the large majority of the outcomes will have been created
- the majority of the resources will have been consumed.

So what information do we need and why do we need it? The answers to this question lie in our needs to:

- establish what work or activities are still outstanding
- record the actual nature of the outcomes
- generate a project history
- check that we achieved what we set out to do.

We undertake these activities so that we can:

- complete the project
- ensure that the client can efficiently manage the operation and maintenance of the project's outcomes
- conduct post-project audits and appraisals.

Project completion

In order to complete the project we need to establish:

- what has been done
- what remains to be done.

Both of these information statements have their roots in the:

- the project specification
- the project change control system.

These, as we saw in Chapter 4, provide us with:

197

- a clear, accessible and unambiguous statement of the project's base line
- an accurate record of the who, why and what of all changes to that specification.

Using these as a starting point we need to physically check what has actually been achieved and then compare this with what should have been achieved. The differences between these will tell us:

- what is left to be done
- what has been done above that which was needed.

The first of these is, initially, the more important. The project manager needs to agree, with the contractors and the client, a programme for completion of this outstanding work and to establish the priority items in that completion programme. Once all of that is done the focus of the project manager's attention will move towards an orderly and well managed closure of the project. On large projects this closure process can almost be a project in itself and for that reason can, as we will see later, be managed by a close-down or termination manager. There can, however, be little doubt that whoever this process is managed by it is made more efficient by the use of close-down check lists. These can add considerably to the ease and efficiency with which this closure process can be conducted; the following is one example.

198

PROJECT CLOSURE CHECK LIST

Activity	Completion date	To be done by
1 Project specification		
A Establish changes to project specification		
B Review and revise specification as required		
2 Project plan		
A Document actual delivery dates		
B Document actual completion dates		
C Hold final project meeting		

Activity	Completion date	To be done by
3 Financial		
A Establish final costs and charges		
B Prepare and issue final financial statement		
4 Work orders and contracts		
A Close all work orders and contracts		
B Prepare contractor reports		
5 Site operations		
A Shut down all site operations		
B Dispose of site equipment		
6 Personnel		
A Update personnel records		
B Complete reassignments		
C Hold final project team meeting		
7 Client		
A Complete project handover		
8 General		
A Complete project report		

Post project audits

We saw in Chapter 12 that an audit can be conducted at any stage of the project's life cycle. The objectives of these audits are to identify:

- the current status of the project
- the potential for project failure
- whether we need to change the way the project is being managed or planned.

However, when we conduct a post-project audit, almost all of the project actions and activities have been completed and the project outcomes are about to be handed over to their legal owners. As a consequence the objectives of the post-project audit are to identify for the client:

- whether or not the project outcomes are complete
- what remains to be done
- whether any cost overruns are justified

and for the project manager:

- whether the budgeted costs were achieved
- whether the project management techniques used were appropriate
- what is to be done with the project assets such as plant and equipment bought for use in the project.

Whether these objectives are answered by a single common audit will, of course, depend upon the nature of the formal relationship between the project manager/team and the client. Where all of these are employed by the same organisation a single audit is not only sensible but also desirable. However, when the project manager/team is employed by a contractor then separate audits will reflect the particular and potentially conflicting needs of both parties. The outcome of the post-project audit consists of a formal report, the size, make-up and focus of which will vary with the cost, nature and outcomes of the project. Large, expensive projects have client audits which are conducted by a team of mixed disciplines and generate extended reports – if only to answer the needs of the shareholders – while the post-project audits of small and limited cost projects can often be generated by a joint project manager/client team and consist of a small report. Projects with outcomes that involve a high level of technical sophistication or require technical expertise which the client may not possess may be audited by independent technical experts. But, whoever conducts this audit and whatever the form of its report, it does need to be stressed that its outcomes are not just a bookkeeping or cost accountancy exercise. They may, for example, reveal defects which are the subject of future legal action between the client and the project organisation. Even when they generate positive conclusions they still may be used in a further exercise to validate, for the client, the expenditure involved or to provide, for the contractor, a basis for a better cost estimating or project control system. As such these post-project audits should be conducted with accuracy and honesty.

200

Post project appraisals

What the post-project audit does not tell us is whether that project has fulfilled the promises which, as we saw in Chapter 3, are often made to justify the sanctioning of the money required for its implementation costs. These estimates of future activities and cash flows may have been concerned with:

■ sales volumes and revenues – as when our project was concerned with the introduction of a new product
■ the performance of plant or equipment – as when our project was concerned with the selection and purchase of a more efficient or faster photocopier
■ the performance of organisations – as when our project was concerned with the centralisation, decentralisation or even re-engineering of our companies
■ the performance of people – as when our project was concerned with the creation of new training schemes.

The post-project appraisal is, without exception, initiated by the project client though it may be conducted, for reasons of impartiality or technical content, by a third party. In large organisations with many projects and high levels of capital expenditure, post-project appraisal is often conducted by a stand-alone department responsible to board level management. The post-project appraisal considers the whole project from its conception through to two or three years after its completion and its objectives are to establish how the project and its outcomes were:

■ reviewed at its proposal stage
■ managed and implemented
■ integrated into the client's operations
■ operated.

The results of this type of review, which will take, for large projects, several months and involve a team of auditors, are presented in the form of a formal report. This report and its conclusions are primarily concerned with improving the organisation's project performance. Examples of how this can be done include:

■ **better cost estimation** – because the estimates are based on historic data and are more accurate
■ **better risk evaluation** – because planning and risk evaluation are based on better data

- **better evaluation of contractors** – because contractor performance is evaluated and monitored more closely
- **better project management** – because better project management tools and more experienced project managers are used.

Managing the transfer of power

We have seen in an earlier chapter that project managers need to be able to:

- lead and motivate teams
- organise the project
- communicate with both the client and the project team
- take decisions.

We have also seen that the authority and power of the project manager will often come about because of the ways in which the above skills are used and a combination of:

- the formal authority of the project manager role
- the personality of the individual.

On a successful project the power of the project manager is used with skill and understanding to:

- empower and enable the project team
- ensure that the resources of the project are used efficiently and effectively.

But by the time this final stage of the project comes around most of the project team will have left and almost all the project's resources will have been consumed, leaving the project manager with a small team and very limited resources to manage. The attention of the client's key project personnel will have shifted towards the problems of the next project or those of getting the outcomes of this project operational.

But does this mean that the role of the project manager has outgrown its value in this final stage? Has he or she become a 'yesterday's person', or is it that the role has merely changed? The answer to this question lies in the fact that the role of the project manager has changed rather than become obsolete. The role of project manager becomes, in this final project stage, one in which the focus of its activities have shifted from:

202

- achieving targets to completing the whole
- broad issues to fine detail
- establishing and maintaining authority to delegating and transferring power.

To achieve this shift effectively requires real skill on the part of the project manager. However, experience tells us that:

- the client may have difficulty in accepting such a radical shift in project manager behaviour
- the project manager may experience difficulty in achieving that shift.

For those reasons it is often worth considering the introduction of:

- a formal ceremony denoting the transfer of authority to the client
- the introduction of a new role – that of a close-down or termination project manager.

However this transfer of power takes place it needs to:

- be conducted with skill
- reflect the reality of the project's end.

Summary

- *The effective and efficient closure of a project can make a significant contribution to the success of that project.*

- *Project closure is the final phase of the project's change process.*

- *The problems of project closure are unique.*

- *Effective and efficient closure is achieved by the careful management of the project's:*
  - *people*
  - *communications*
  - *information*
  - *power structure.*

- *Post-project audits:*
  - *can be conducted by both client and project team*
  - *are concerned with identifying:*
    the degree of completion of the project outcomes
    the costs involved in generating those outcomes
    the effectiveness and relevance of the project management techniques used.

■ *Post-project appraisals should:*
  – *be conducted by the client*
  – *examine the whole project*
  – *start at the project's conception and finish at the end of two years of outcome operation.*

14

Key points for successful projects

Overview

We have now looked at all of the factors which go to make a successful project. This, the final chapter of this book, is a review of the key points contained in all of the previous chapters.

Objectives

By the end of this chapter you should:
- **have been reminded of the key points**
- **have identified what you have learnt by reading this book**
- **decided how you are going to manage your projects in the future.**

Condensed key points

Project definition

A project is a sequence of activities which are:

- connected
- conducted over a limited period of time
- targeted to generate a unique but well defined outcome.

All projects:

- involve people
- are unique
- are concerned with change
- have defined outcomes and end-points
- use a variety of transitory resources

- have a life cycle with the following stages:
  - conception
  - birth and development
  - adulthood
  - old age and termination.

Risk and uncertainty

All projects involve risk and uncertainty but these can be reduced by:

- identifying the type, level and source of foreseeable risks
- taking necessary steps (if possible) to reduce or eliminate those risks
- deciding whether or not to accept those risks.

Project choice

Selecting the 'right' project is a key first step towards a successful project. Projects can be chosen by numerical or non-numerical methods, including:

- ranking
- payback
- rate of return
- NPV
- internal rate of return.

Project organisation

The effective project organisation will balance the conflicting needs of:

- the client
- the project team
- the project.

The main types of project organisation are:

- client focused organisation
- matrix organisation
- project focused organisation.

Choosing which of these is right for your project involves:

- judgement
- knowledge of what has worked in the past

- a good understanding of the nature of the project outcomes, risks, costs, duration and special technology or knowledge needs.

The first and essential step towards organising your project involves the generation of the project:

- specification
- roles and responsibility definitions
- budget and accounting procedures
- change control procedures.

Project plans

The project plan is the mechanism which enables us to convert project objectives into concrete realities. A successful project plan needs the skills and abilities of people to make it come to life. The first step in creating a plan is to list:

- the actions needed
- completion and start times
- people and resources needed.

207

Project plans can be:

- Gantt charts
- activity on arrow (AOA) networks
- activity on node (AON) networks.

Managing the project

The role of the project manager:

- is demanding and stimulating
- requires a rare mix of skills and abilities
- is a key factor in the success of a project.

The primary task of this role is the efficient and effective management of the ways in which the objectives of the project are attained.

The project manager must be able to:

- integrate rather than divide
- provide the means rather than oversee
- see the 'big picture' rather then the detailed tunnel vision view.

Project managers must be able to:

- lead and motivate teams
- communicate
- organise the required resources, people and information
- take decisions.

Project teams

A good project team is essential to a successful project. Project teams are different to groups, and their members:

- have shared purposes
- undertake co-operative action
- generate collective outcomes
- create defined, measurable team 'products'.

Effective project teams usually have between six and eight members with a maximum size of ten.

The teams of successful projects go through stages of development with different ambiences and levels of productivity.

Project team members behave in ways which are influenced by:

- the project task
- the behaviour of other team members.

Project team members should be chosen for:

- their functional skills
- their decision making and problem solving skills
- their skills in working with other team members.

Project estimates and budgets

The creation of accurate cost estimates and an accurate budget is a vital factor in the success of the project. Types of estimate are:

- ball park estimate (± 30 per cent)
- feasibility estimate (± 15–25 per cent)
- definitive estimate (± 5–10 per cent).

Estimates must include:

- labour costs
- material costs

- equipment costs
- insurance, tax and other charges
- inflation allowance
- contingency allowance.

Estimating techniques include:

- exponential method
- learning curves
- activity profiles
- factorial estimating.

Budgets are plans for money usage. Budgets enable projects to be:

- monitored
- controlled.

Projects and change

209

The effective management of the change which is an integral element of the project's structure is a key to the success of the project.

The change which the project exists to create is generally but not exclusively:

- significant
- irreversible.

The change of the project needs to be managed with care and thought, using tools such as force field analysis, and by a co-ordinated and balanced use of the factors of:

- people
- communication
- information
- power.

Effective management of the change that projects create:

- accepts and works with the resistance that people have to change
- accepts and works with conflict
- involves those affected by the change
- generates their commitment.

Project problem solving

Projects have problems which:

■ can be about any aspect of the project
■ can have a wide range of possible causes and an equally wide range of solutions.

Project problems are solved by:

■ collecting and analysing information
■ identifying the real problem
■ generating alternative solutions
■ choosing which alternative to implement.

Information on project problems can be collected by:

■ diagramming
■ sampling
■ ratioing

and analysed by using:

■ averages, medians or modes
■ moving averages
■ decision trees.

Alternative solutions can be generated by:

■ brainstorming
■ lateral thinking

and evaluated by:

■ the Delphi method
■ ranking.

Project conflicts

Conflicts occur in all of our projects with both good and bad effects. Project conflicts are about the often opposing interests and needs of:

■ the client
■ the project
■ the project team.

These project conflicts have, at their core, the issues of:

- influence
- authority
- autonomy.

Conflicts can be resolved and managed by:

- avoidance or dispersion/defusion
- containment or confrontation.

The choice of conflict management style depends upon:

- circumstance
- context
- preference.

Accepting and managing conflict leads to:

- increased trust and risk taking
- win-win situations.

Ignoring or suppressing conflict generates:

- low levels of trust and openness
- frustration
- lose-win, win-lose or lose-lose situations.

211

Negotiations can be used to achieve win-win situations; they occur throughout the whole of the project life cycle. Effective negotiations require skill and ability from all involved.

Monitoring and controlling projects

The effective and efficient use of the processes of monitoring and controlling are essential to project success. Project monitoring involves:

- measuring
- collecting
- recording
- collating
- analysing information.

Monitoring is based on:

- the project plan
- the project budget.

Monitoring can use:

- project milestones
- S curves
- progress reports
- limit testing
- earned value analysis
- project meetings.

Controlling the project is aimed at reducing the gap between what is happening and what we had planned should happen.

The successful project is controlled by:

- measuring or monitoring what is happening
- comparing it to what should be happening
- adjusting the project inputs in ways which reflect the size and polarity of the difference.

Project closure

212

The effective and efficient closure of a project can make a significant contribution to the success of that project. Project closure is the final phase of the project's change process and, as such, has unique problems. Effective and efficient closure is achieved by the careful management of the project's:

- people
- communications
- information
- power structure.

Post-project audits:

- can be conducted by both client and project team
- are concerned with identifying:
  - the degree of completion of the project outcomes
  - the costs involved in generating those outcomes
  - the effectiveness and relevance of the project management techniques used.

Post-project appraisals should:

- be conducted by the client
- examine the whole project
- start at the project's conception and review at least two years of outcome operation.

CAN YOU MANAGE A SUCCESSFUL PROJECT?

Under each of the headings below ring a number which is nearest to what you would feel when managing a project and then add up your total.

I measure everything	1 2 3 4 5 6 7	I monitor the key aspects of the project.
I always lead my team the same way.	1 2 3 4 5 6 7	I try to work out which way will work best for this team and this project.
We pay them – isn't that enough?	1 2 3 4 5 6 7	I see my team as creative problem solvers.
As project manager I tell people what I think.	1 2 3 4 5 6 7	I listen when people talk and they listen when I talk.
Planning is a waste of time.	1 2 3 4 5 6 7	Plans provide a strong basis for management decisions.
My team makes limited contributions and no dissent is expressed.	1 2 3 4 5 6 7	Everyone is fully engaged and effectively used.
I resist change and fight it all the way.	1 2 3 4 5 6 7	Change is an opportunity to be grasped.

213

Conflict is bad and should be suppressed.	1 2 3 4 5 6 7	Conflict can be good if managed well.
When I negotiate I try to rip off the other side.	1 2 3 4 5 6 7	I try to get a deal which is right for everyone.
Project close-down is a boring task to be given to a junior team member.	1 2 3 4 5 6 7	Closing down a project is as important as its start-up.

Key:

Total

10–30	You can't be serious!
30–50	Well done – a good score and a strong basis to build on.
50–70	Excellent – now go and do it.

214

Conclusion

The perfect project manager has yet to be born and we all manage our projects with differing degrees of proficiency and capability. And yet, this is the way it ought to be for we, like our projects, are unique and individual – each with a singular and personal 'kit bag' of skills, experience and abilities. The purpose of this book has not been to create or engender a race of clone-like 'super' project managers but to enable the many managers who use the powerful tool of the project to do so more effectively. The way that you, as an individual, manage your projects is something that cannot be brought down from some high mountain engraved on tablets of stone – it is something that you will define, explore, change, refine and even reinvent as you manage those projects. My hope is that this book has enabled you to start or continue that process and that you have enjoyed reading it as much as I have enjoyed writing it. Have fun with your projects!

Glossary of project terms

■

activity a basic component of a project plan which takes time and uses resources.

activity on arrow or **AOA network** a method of planning projects which uses arrows to represent activities.

activity on node or **AON network** a method of planning projects which uses nodes to represent activities.

ACWP actual cost of work performed.

bar chart *see* Gantt chart.

BCWP budgeted cost of work performed.

BCWS budgeted cost of work scheduled.

budget the original estimated cost of the project built up from estimates of activity labour, material and equipment needs.

client focus project organisation a type of project organisation in which project activities are integrated into the structure of the client organisation.

cost variance the difference between the budgeted cost of the work performed and the actual cost of that work.

critical path the sequence of activities that leads to the shortest project completion time.

dependency *see* interdependency.

dummy a connection in an AOA network which has zero duration and doesn't represent an activity but does indicate interdependency.

estimate an approximate judgement, based on probability, of the cost or size of resources needed for a project task or activity.

event the beginning or end of an activity.

EET the earliest time by which an event can occur.

float the difference between the time required for an activity and the time available.

Gantt chart a method of project planning which represents activities by the use of horizontal bars where the length is proportional to the calendar time required for the activity.

interdependency when an activity cannot be started until a prior activity has finished.

internal rate of return the interest rate at which the project's net present value (NPV) is zero.

LET latest event time.

matrix organisation a type of project organisation in which project team members report to both their functional boss and their project boss.

milestones significant points in a project.

net present value or **NPV** the sum of the capital required to implement the project and the present values of the estimated future profits of a defined number of years.

node a connection point in a project planning network. In an AOA network it is the beginning or end of an activity, in an AON network it is the activity itself.

payback period the time from the start of the project to the point at which the project's cumulative cash flow is zero.

profitability index the ratio of the NPV of the project to the capital required for its implementation.

project a sequence of activities which are:
– connected
– conducted over a limited period of time
– targeted to generate a unique but well defined outcome.

project characteristics
– people-centred
– unique
– limited and defined life span
– concerned with change
– defined outcomes
– use a variety of resources.

project focus project organisation a type of project organisation in which the project team exists as a stand-alone organisation, separate from the client organisation.

project inputs
– information
– people
– resources.

project key dimensions
- cost
- time
- performance
- quality.

project life cycle
- conception
- birth and development
- adulthood
- old age and termination.

project specification the source of definitive information about a project's scope, goals and objectives, organisation, budget and justification.

rate of return annual profit/implementation cost × 100%.

ranking a non-numerate method of choosing between alternative projects by generating the sum of each alternative's rankings, relative to others, under a number of criteria.

resource something needed in order to do work, such as money, equipment, people, information, skill, knowledge and materials.

risk the estimated degree of uncertainty.

schedule variance the difference between the budgeted cost of the work performed and the budget cost of the work scheduled to have been performed.

slack *see* float.

uncertainty the lack of information about the duration, occurrence or value of future events.

variance the difference between estimated or budgeted costs and actual costs (*see also* cost variance and schedule variance).

Index

■

Dear Pitman Publishing Customer

IMPORTANT – Please Read This Now!

We are delighted to announce a special free service for all of our customers.

Simply complete this form and return it to the FREEPOST address overleaf to receive:

A Free Customer Newsletter

B Free Information Service

C Exclusive Customer Offers – which have included free software, videos and relevant products

D Opportunity to take part in product development sessions

E The chance for you to write about your own business experience and become one of our respected authors

Fill this in now and return it to us (no stamp needed in the UK) to join our customer information service.

Name: Position:

Company/Organisation:

Address (including postcode):

                                                   Country:

Telephone: Fax:

Nature of business:

Title of book purchased:

ISBN (printed on back cover): [0] [2] [7] [3] [ ] [ ] [ ] [ ] [ ]

Comments:

- | **Fold Here Then Staple Once** | -

We would be very grateful if you could answer these questions to help us with market research.

1 Where/How did you hear of this book?

[ ] in a bookshop

[ ] in a magazine/newspaper

(please state which):

[ ] information through the post

[ ] recommendation from a colleague

[ ] other (please state which):

2 Where did you buy this book

[ ] Direct from Pitman Publishing

[ ] From a bookclub

[ ] From a bookshop (state which)

3 Which newspaper(s)/magazine(s) do you read regularly?:

4 When buying a business book which factors influence you most?

(Please rank in order)

[ ] recommendation from a colleague

[ ] price

[ ] content

[ ] recommendation in a bookshop

[ ] author

[ ] publisher

[ ] title

[ ] other(s):

5 Is this book a

[ ] personal purchase?

[ ] company purchase?

6 Would you be prepared to spend a few minutes talking to our customer services staff to help with product development? YES/NO

The Business Publisher

Written for managers competing in today's tough business world, our books will give you a competitive edge by showing you how to:

● increase quality, efficiency and productivity throughout your organisation
● use both proven and innovative management techniques
● improve your management skills and those of your staff
● implement winning customer strategies

In short they provide concise, practical information that you can use every